# Learn Java by Association with
## C • COBOL • FORTRAN PASCAL • VISUAL BASIC

**A PRACTICAL DICTIONARY OF PROGRAMMING LANGUAGES**

**Dilip Dedhia**

**Publisher**
Engineering Mechanics Technology, Inc.
4340 Stevens Creek Blvd. #166
San Jose, CA 95129
info@techednet.com

For information on book distributions outside of US, or to arrange for bulk purchase discounts for sales promotions, book clubs or fund-raisers, please contact the publisher at the above address.

© 2000 Engineering Mechanics Technology, Inc. All rights reserved. No part of this book may be reproduced, in any form or by any means, without permission in writing from the publisher.

Library of Congress Card Number: 00-190272

ISBN 0-9679469-0-5

Printed in the United States of America

First Printing: March 2000

The author and the publisher have used their best efforts at preparing this book. These efforts include testing the theory and programs in this book. However, the author and publisher make no warranty of any kind, expressed or implied, with regard to these programs or the documentation contained in this book. The author and publisher shall not be liable for any incidental or consequential damages in connection with, or arising out of, the performance or use of these programs or any information contained in this book.

Trademarked names appear throughout this book. Rather than list the names and entities that own the trademarks or insert a trademark symbol with each mention of the trademarked name, the publisher states that it is using the names for editorial purposes only and to the benefit of the trademark owner, with no intention of infringing upon the trademark.

## PREFACE

Welcome to the *Learn Java by Association with C, Cobol, Fortran, Pascal, Visual Basic*. This book developed from the author's experience teaching the Java programming language to those who already know some other programming language. The present compilation has been put together from the user's point of view. It is intended to help programmers learn a new programming language by association – by looking at a familiar language that they already know and quickly seeing how the same tasks can be performed in Java. To that end, this is a collection of basic language features rather than a comprehensive comparison of the programming languages. Although the main goal of the book is to teach Java from the knowledge of either C, Visual Basic, Fortran, Cobol or Pascal, the book can also be used to quickly learn the basic syntax of any language included in the book.

## HOW THE BOOK IS ORGANIZED

The book contains 50 sections and each section is spread over four pages. The first two pages of each section contain Fortran, Visual Basic, C and Java, and the next two pages contain Cobol, Pascal and Java. Java is duplicated on both of these pages to make it convenient to compare with any of the languages considered in the book. Following is a sample layout for each section:

▶ ▶▶

| Operators | | Operators | |
|---|---|---|---|
| FORTRAN | Visual Basic | C | Java |
| | | | |

◀◀ ■

| Operators | Operators | |
|---|---|---|
| Cobol | Pascal | Java |
| | | |

## SOURCE CODE AND UPDATES

For the source code of all the examples in this book and updates to the book, please visit **www.TechEdNet.com**.

## ABOUT THE AUTHOR

Dilip Dedhia is an instructor at the University of California, Santa Cruz Extension in Santa Clara. He has been programming for 20 years and has been teaching Java and Visual Basic since 1995. He is also President of Engineering Mechanics Technology, Inc., and holds a Ph.D. from Oregon Graduate Institute of Science and Technology (1980).

## ACKNOWLEDGEMENTS

I would like to thank Dr. David Harris for the initial discussion regarding the book project, which encouraged me to go forward with the book. The format of the book was also suggested by him. The C code in the book was developed by Sai Chintalapudi, the Pascal code by Patrick Smith and the Cobol code by Pradip Joshi, and I am thankful to them for providing the code in an efficient manner. My special thanks to John Grogan and Kamal Hyder for doing a careful technical review of the book. The description of the book that appears on the back cover is also based on suggestions by John Grogan. Finally I would like to thank Rinki Dedhia and Reesha Dedhia for proofing the manuscript.

# Table of Contents

1. Compiling and Running Programs ..... 2
2. A Program that Prints `Hello World` on the Console ..... 6
3. General Comments ..... 10
4. Comments in the Source Code ..... 14
5. List of Keywords ..... 18
6. Primitive Data Types ..... 22
7. Declaring and Initializing Variables ..... 26
8. Operators – Arithmetic ..... 30
9. Operators – Relational ..... 34
10. Operators – Bitwise and Boolean ..... 38
11. Operator Precedence ..... 42
12. Decision Making with `if` Statement ..... 46
13. Decision Making with `if...else` Statement ..... 50
14. Decision Making with `if...elseif...else` Statement ..... 54
15. Decision Making with `if...elseif...else` Statement - Example ..... 58
16. Decision Making with `switch`, `Select Case`, `Evaluate` or `case () of` Statements ..... 62
17. Decision Making with `switch`, `Select Case`, `Evaluate` or `case() of` Statements – Example 1 ..... 66
18. Decision Making with `switch`, `Select Case,Evaluate` or `case()of` Statements – Example 2 ..... 70
19. Looping Statements – Pre-test, Indeterminate – `while, perform until` ..... 74
20. Looping Statements – Post-test, Indeterminate – `do while, repeat` ..... 78
21. Looping Statements – Determinate – `do ..enddo, for, for...next, perform times` ..... 82
22. Looping Statements – Nested, Determinate – `do...enddo, for, for...next, perform times` ..... 86
23. Nested Loops – Ways of Terminating ..... 90
24. Other Ways of Making a Selection ..... 94
25. Read/Write from the Console ..... 98
26. Write to a Sequential File ..... 102
27. Read from a Sequential File ..... 106
28. Read/Write from a Binary Random File ..... 110
29. Define and use a Method (Function) ..... 114
30. Method (Function) with one Parameter and Return Value - Example ..... 118
31. Method (Function) with Two Parameters and Return Value - Example ..... 122
32. Built-in Math Functions ..... 126
33. Math Functions – Examples ..... 130

34. Converting Strings to Numeric Types .................................................................................................... 134
35. String Operations – Returning a Substring .......................................................................................... 138
36. String Operations – Searching within a String for a Sequence of Characters .................................... 142
37. String Operations – Replacing Character within a String with a new Character ............................... 146
38. Date and Time Functions ..................................................................................................................... 150
39. Date and Time Functions - Example ................................................................................................... 154
40. One Dimensional Arrays ...................................................................................................................... 158
41. Two Dimensional Arrays ...................................................................................................................... 162
42. Copying an Array ................................................................................................................................. 166
43. Formatting Numeric Output ................................................................................................................. 170
44. Converting between Different Data Types ......................................................................................... 174
45. Passing Arrays to Functions ................................................................................................................ 178
46. Program to Read Numbers from a Text File ....................................................................................... 182
47. Program to Sort Numbers Using Shell Sort Algorithm ....................................................................... 186
48. Program to Compute the Leap Year .................................................................................................... 190
49. Program to Generate Lotto Numbers .................................................................................................. 194
50. Program to Generate Character-based Bar Graph .............................................................................. 198

This page intentionally left blank.

## 1. Compiling and Running Programs

| FORTRAN | Visual Basic |
|---|---|
| Microsoft Fortran Power Station 4.0 was used for all the examples in this book. All the examples in this book involve one source file, however, large applications can have multiple source files. | Microsoft Visual Basic Professional version 6 was used for all the examples in this book. Since the focus of this book is on the language syntax and logic, minimum user interface elements were used in the Visual Basic projects. |

**Steps for creating and running a program** (FORTRAN)

- Create the source code (for example, `ABC.FOR`) using a text editor, like Notepad.

- Save the file with `.FOR` extension.

- Compile the file as

    `FL32 ABC.FOR`

- The compiler will produce a binary executable file named `ABC.EXE`

- Run the program by typing the name of the .exe file at the console

    `ABC`

This step will run the program.

**Steps for creating and running a program** (Visual Basic)

- Most examples in this book involve starting Visual Basic and drawing a `CommandButton` instance (`Command1`) on the Form. The code is then placed within the click event of the button which can be reached by double-clicking on the button. In some cases, a `TextBox` instance is also used.

- To run the project, simply click on the Start button from the toolbar or use Start item from the Run menu.

- An executable can be created using the Make EXE item from the File menu.

## Compiling and Running Programs

| C | Java |
|---|---|
| All the C code examples in this book were tested with Microsoft Visual Studio 6. However, all the examples are written in generic C and can be easily compiled using any C compiler on any operating system.<br><br>**Steps for creating and running a program**<br><br>- Open Microsoft Visual C++, create a source file and save it as `Abc.c`<br>- From the **Build** menu, select **Build.**<br>- If prompted for the workspace, select yes.<br>- Select "**Execute..**" from the **Build** menu to run the program. | JDK 2 SDK 1.2.2, downloaded from java.sun.com was used for all the examples in this book. All the examples in this book involve one java class in one file, however, large applications can have multiple classes in multiple files.<br><br>**Steps for creating and running a program**<br><br>- Create the source code (for example, `Abc.java` containing class `Abc`) using a text editor, like Notepad.<br>- Save the file with `.java` extension.<br>- Compile the file as<br><br>  `javac Abc.java`<br><br>  The compiler will produce a binary file named `Abc.class` No other compilation or linking steps are required.<br><br>- Run the program by using the java interpreter as<br><br>  `java Abc`<br><br>  This step will run the main method from `Abc` class. |

## Compiling and Running Programs

### COBOL

Fujitsu Cobol 3.0 was used for all the examples in this book. The compiler is available for free from www.adtools.com/download. All the examples in this book involve one source file, however, large applications can have multiple source files.

**Steps for creating and running a program**

- Create the source code (for example, `ABC.COB`) using a text editor, like Notepad.

- Save the file with `.COB` extension.

- Compile the file running `WINCOB.EXE` (the Cobol compiler), which will produce `ABC.OBJ` file.

- Link the ABC.OBJ file using the `WINLINK.EXE` (the Cobol linker)

- The linker will produce a binary executable file named `ABC.EXE`

- Run the program by typing the name of the .exe file at the console

    `ABC`

This step will run the program.

## Compiling and Running Programs

| PASCAL | Java |
|---|---|
| Borland Delphi 4 from Inprise was used for all Pascal examples. Although the Delphi Integrated Design Environment (IDE) is intended to be used primarily for developing Windows applications, it can also generate console applications with the use of the `{$APPTYPE CONSOLE}` pre-processor directive.<br><br>**Steps for creating and running a program**<br><br>- Create the source code (for example, `Abc.pas` containing the Abc program) using a text editor, like Notepad.<br><br>- Save the file with .pas extension.<br><br>- Compile the file as<br><br>  `dcc32 Abc.pas`<br><br>No other compilation or linking steps are required. All linked libraries are declared in the uses clause of the program and the compiler links the necessary modules automatically.<br><br>- The compiler will produce an executable as `Abc.exe`.<br><br>- Run the program by typing `Abc` at the command prompt. | JDK 2 SDK 1.2.2, downloaded from java.sun.com was used for all the examples in this book. All the examples in this book involve one java class in one file, however, large applications can have multiple classes in multiple files.<br><br>**Steps for creating and running a program**<br><br>- Create the source code (for example, `Abc.java` containing class `Abc`) using a text editor, like Notepad.<br><br>- Save the file with `.java` extension.<br><br>- Compile the file as<br><br>  `javac Abc.java`<br><br>  The compiler will produce a binary file named `Abc.class` No other compilation or linking steps are required.<br><br>- Run the program by using the java interpreter as<br><br>  `java Abc`<br><br>This step will run the main method from `Abc` class. |

## 2. A Program that Prints `Hello World` on the Console

| FORTRAN | Visual Basic |
|---|---|
| ```
Program HW
write(*,*) 'Hello World!'
stop
end
``` | ```
Private Sub Command1_Click()
MsgBox "Hello World!"
End Sub
``` |
| Create a file `HW.for` using the Notepad editor.<br>To compile the program, at the DOS prompt, type<br>    `f132 HW.for`<br>The compiler will create a file called `HW.exe`<br>To run the program, type<br><br>    `HW`<br><br>"Hello World!" would be displayed on the console<br><br>In the following screenshot, you type the commands that are boldfaced:<br><br>```
C:\book>f132 hw.for

C:\book>HW
Hello World!
Stop - Program terminated.
``` | Start Visual Basic, select a `CommandButton` control from the toolbox and draw an instance on the form.<br><br>Double-click on the command button to get to the code window. Within the template provided, type in the following code.<br><br>`MsgBox "Hello World!"`<br><br>To run the project, simply click on the Start button from the toolbar or use Start item from the Run menu.<br><br>A message box with the string "Hello World!" and an OK button will be displayed. |
```

## A Program that Prints `Hello World` on the Console

| C | Java |
|---|---|
| ```c<br>#include <stdio.h><br>int main()<br>{<br>   printf("Hello World!");<br>   printf("\n");<br>   return 0;<br>}<br>``` | ```java<br>public class HW{<br>   public static void main(String sargs[]){<br>      System.out.println("Hello World!");<br>   }<br>}<br>``` |
| A text file containing the above code was added to an empty MS Visual C++ project. The program was compiled to `HelloWorld.exe`<br><br>The program was run at the DOS prompt as follows:<br><br>In the following screenshot, you type the commands that are boldfaced:<br><br>```<br>C:\book>HelloWorld<br><br>Hello World!<br><br>C:\book><br>``` | Create a file `HW.java` using the Notepad editor.<br>To compile the program, at the DOS prompt, type<br><br>`javac HW.java`<br><br>The compiler will create a file called `HW.class`<br><br>To run the program, type<br><br>`java HW`<br><br>"Hello World!" would be displayed on the console<br><br>In the following screenshot, you type the commands that are boldfaced:<br><br>```<br>C:\book>javac HW.java<br><br>C:\book>java HW<br>Hello World!<br><br>C:\book><br>``` |

## A Program that Prints Hello World on the Console

### COBOL

```cobol
       IDENTIFICATION DIVISION.
      *---------------------------------------
           PROGRAM-ID.              AbcP.
      *---------------------------------------
      *   This is a sample program
      *    which displays
      *    'Hello World' on console.
      $PAGE "WORKING STORAGE Section"
       DATA DIVISION.
      *---------------------------------------
       WORKING-STORAGE SECTION.
      *---------------------------------------

       01 DISPLAY-STRING    PIC X(80) VALUE
           "Hello World!".
      *---------------------------------------
       PROCEDURE DIVISION.
      *---------------------------------------

       0000-MAIN.
      *---------
               DISPLAY SPACES.
               DISPLAY DISPLAY-STRING.
            STOP RUN.
       0000-EXIT. EXIT.
```

## A Program that Prints `Hello World` on the Console

| PASCAL | Java |
|---|---|
| ```<br>program HW;<br>{$APPTYPE CONSOLE}<br>begin<br>  Writeln('Hello World!');<br>end.<br>``` | ```<br>public class HW{<br>  public static void main(String sargs[]){<br>      System.out.println("Hello World!");<br>  }<br>}<br>``` |

| | |
|---|---|
| Create a file `HW.pas` using the Notepad editor.<br><br>To compile the progam, at the DOS prompt type<br><br>`dcc32 HW.pas`<br><br>The compiler will create a file called HW.exe<br><br>To run the program, type<br><br>`HW`<br><br>"Hello World!" would be displayed on the console<br><br>In the following screenshot, you type the commands that are boldfaced:<br><br><pre>c:\book>**dcc32 HW.pas**<br><br>c:\book>**HW**<br><br>Hello World!<br><br>c:\book></pre> | Create a file `HW.java` using the Notepad editor.<br>To compile the program, at the DOS prompt, type<br><br>`javac HW.java`<br><br>The compiler will create a file called `HW.class`<br><br>To run the program, type<br><br>`java HW`<br><br>"Hello World!" would be displayed on the console<br><br>In the following screenshot, you type the commands that are boldfaced:<br><br><pre>C:\book>**javac HW.java**<br><br>C:\book>**java HW**<br>Hello World!<br><br>C:\book></pre> |

## 3. General Comments

| FORTRAN | Visual Basic |
|---|---|
| Fortran is case-insensitive. | Visual Basic is case-insensitive. |
| Fortran statements do not have termination character. | Visual Basic supports object orientation. |
| Fortran continuation character is C in the 6$^{th}$ column. | Visual Basic statements do not have termination character. |
| Program execution starts with `Program progName`. | Visual Basic statements can continue on more than one line by the use of the continuation characters (space followed by an underscore). Multiple statements can be placed on the same line if separated by colon(:). |
| | Program execution starts either with `Sub Main()` or with the `Load` event of the specified form. |

**General Comments**

| C | Java |
|---|---|
| C is a case-sensitive language. | Java is a case-sensitive language. |
| Global variables and global functions are supported in C | Java does not have global variables or global functions. |
| C statements are terminated with a semi-colon(;) | Java is a completely object-oriented language. |
| C program execution starts at the main() function. | Functions defined within a class are called either member functions or methods. |
| | In a Java application, program execution starts at the main method. |
| | Java does not support pointer arithmetic. |
| | Java statements are terminated with a semi-colon(;). |
| | By convention, { is placed at the end of a line, unlike in C where it is placed on a new line. |

**General Comments**

## COBOL

The Cobol programs are written according to a special structure that is organized into a hierarchy of parts. Columns 1 through 6 contain a sequence number. Column 7 is called the indicator area, and is reserved for a hyphen used as a continuation character. A * (star) in this column indicates that the line contains a comment entry. Columns 8 through 72 contain Cobol source code.

Every Cobol program consists of four divisions in the following order:

```
IDENTIFICATION DIVISION
ENVIRONMENT DIVISION
DATA DIVISION
PROCEDURE DIVISION.
```

In Cobol, all the variables are global variables.

A Cobol program always start executing from PROCEDURE DIVISION.

In Cobol, the statements are always terminated with a period (.).

Cobol is not a case-sensitive Language.

## General Comments

| PASCAL | Java |
|---|---|
| Pascal is a case-insensitive language. | Java is a case-sensitive language. |
| Pascal does have global variables and global functions. | Java does not have global variables or global functions. |
| Pascal is an Object enabled structured programming language. | Java is a completely object-oriented language. |
| Functions within a class are called member `functions` or methods. They are designated by the keywords function if they return a value (or object), or `procedure` if they have no return type. | Functions defined within a class are called either member functions or methods. |
| In a Pascal application, program execution starts at the `program` keyword. | In a Java application, program execution starts at the main method. |
| Pascal does support pointer arithmetic. | Java does not support pointer arithmetic. |
| Pascal statements are terminated with a semi-colon(;). | Java statements are terminated with a semi-colon(;). |
| | By convention, { is placed at the end of a line, unlike in C where it is placed on a new line. |

## 4. Comments in the Source Code

| FORTRAN | Visual Basic |
|---|---|
| In a Fortran source file, any line beginning with C or * in the first column is considered a comment line and ignored by the compiler. Columns 1-5 can contain a numeric label, any character in column 6 is interpreted as a statement continuation, columns 7-72 contain Fortran statements. Anything in column 73 and beyond is ignored.<br><br>Example:<br><br>```      x = 3      y = 10c     this is a comment line      z = 21``` | There are three ways of commenting the source code:<br><br>Comments start with either the REM keyword or with a single quote (')<br><br>```REM This is one type of comment' this is also a comment```<br><br>Comments can also appear at the end of a statement as in the following example:<br><br>```int x = 3 ' set x to three```<br><br>Visual Basic does not have multiline comments. |

## Comments in the Source Code

| C | Java |
|---|---|
| There are two ways of commenting the source code:<br><br>1. Single line comment, starts with //<br><br>`// This is one type of comment`<br>`int x = 3; // set x to 3`<br><br>2. Multiline comment – begins with /* and ends with */<br><br>`/* This program computes`<br>`the sum and product of the numbers,`<br>`given integer inputs`<br>`*/` | There are three ways of commenting the source code:<br><br>1. Single line comment, starts with //<br><br>`// This is one type of comment`<br>`int x = 3; // set x to 3`<br><br>2. Multiline comment – begins with /* and ends with */<br><br>`/* This program computes`<br>`the sum and product of the numbers,`<br>`given integer inputs`<br>`*/`<br><br>3. Multiline documenting comment - begins with /** and ends with */. The documenting comments can be used to generate html documentation of your source code using the `javadoc` program (part of the JDK)<br><br>`/** This method computes`<br>`the sum and product of the numbers,`<br>`given integer inputs`<br>`*/` |

## Comments in the Source Code

### COBOL

A comment in source program is indicated by specifying ' * ' in column 7 of the source code. The compiler will ignore the lines containing * in column 7.

Example: The first 4 lines are comment lines.

```
*******************************
* This routine validates the
* date-entered
*******************************
  DATE-VALIDATE.
```

## Comments in the Source Code

| PASCAL | Java |
|---|---|
| There two ways of commenting the source code:<br><br>1. Single line comments, starts with //<br><br>`// This is one type of comment`<br>`x : Integer = 3;  // set x to 3`<br><br>2. Multiline comment – begins with { and ends with }<br><br>`{ This program computes`<br>`the sum and product of the numbers,`<br>`given the integer inputs`<br>`}`<br><br>Note: Pre-processor directives are bracketed by {$...} | There are three ways of commenting the source code:<br><br>1. Single line comment, starts with //<br><br>`// This is one type of comment`<br>`int x = 3; // set x to 3`<br><br>2. Multiline comment – begins with /* and ends with */<br><br>`/* This program computes`<br>`the sum and product of the numbers,`<br>`given integer inputs`<br>`*/`<br><br>3. Multiline documenting comment - begins with /** and ends with */. The documenting comments can be used to generate html documentation of your source code using the `javadoc` program (part of the JDK)<br><br>`/** This method computes`<br>`the sum and product of the numbers,`<br>`given integer inputs`<br>`*/` |

## 5. List of Keywords

| FORTRAN | Visual Basic |
|---|---|

Fortran does not have reserved words like most other programming languages. It is, however, recommended that the use of Fortran statements as names of variables or functions should be avoided.

Certain compilers may enforce certain words as reserved.

| | | | |
|---|---|---|---|
| As | Binary | ByRef | ByVal |
| Date | Else | Empty | Error |
| False | For | Friend | Get |
| Input | Is | Len | Let |
| Lock | Me | Mid | New |
| Next | Nothing | Null | On |
| Option | Optional | ParamArray | Print |
| Private | Property | Public | Resume |
| Seek | Set | Static | Step |
| String | Then | Time | To |
| True | WithEvents | | |

## List of Keywords

### C

| | | | |
|---|---|---|---|
| auto | break | case | char |
| const | continue | default | do |
| double | else | enum | extern |
| float | for | goto | if |
| int | long | register | return |
| short | signed | sizeof | static |
| struct | switch | typedef | union |
| unsigned | void | volatile | while |

### Java

| | | | |
|---|---|---|---|
| abstract | boolean | break | byte |
| case | catch | char | class |
| const | continue | default | do |
| double | else | extends | false |
| final | finally | float | for |
| goto | if | implements | import |
| inner | instanceof | int | interface |
| long | native | new | null |
| operator | package | private | protected |
| public | return | short | static |
| strictfp | super | switch | synchronized |
| this | throw | throws | transient |
| true | try | void | volatile |
| while | | | |

## List of Keywords

# COBOL

| ACCEPT | ACCESS | ADD | ADVANCING | AFTER | ALL | ALPHABET | ALPHABETIC | ALPHABETIC-LOWER | ALPHABETIC-UPPER |
|---|---|---|---|---|---|---|---|---|---|
| ALPHANUMERIC | ALPHANUMERIC-EDITED | ALSO | ALTER | ALTERNATE | AND | ANY | ARE | AREA | AREAS |
| ASCENDING | ASSIGNIN | AT | AUTHOR | BEFORE | BINARY | BLANK | BLOCK | BOTTOM | BY |
| CALL | CANCEL | CD | CF | CH | CHARACTER | CHARACTERS | CLASS | CLOSE | CODE |
| CODE-SET | COLLATING | COLUMN | COMMA | COMMON | COMMUNICATION | COMP | COMPUTATIONAL | COMPUTE | CONFIGURATION |
| CONTAINS | CONTENT | CONTINUE | CONTROL | CONTROLS | CONVERTING | COPY | CORR | CORRESPONDING | COUNT |
| CURRENCY | DATA | DATE | DATE-COMPILED | DATE-WRITTEN | DAY | DAY-OF-WEEK | DE | DEBUG-CONTENTS | DEBUG-ITEM |
| DEBUG-LINE | DEBUG-NAME | DEBUG-SUB-1 | DEBUG-SUB-2 | DEBUG-SUB-3 | DEBUGGING | DECIMAL-POINT | DECLARATIVES | DELETE | DELIMITED |
| DELIMITER | DEPENDING | DESCENDING | DESTINATION | DETAIL | DISABLE | DISPLAY | DIVIDE | DIVISION | DOWN |
| DUPLICATES | DYNAMIC | EGI | ELSE | EMI | ENABLE | END | END-ADD | END-CALL | END-COMPUTE |
| END-DELETE | END-DIVIDE | END-EVALUATE | END-IF | END-MULTIPLY | END-OF-PAGE | END-PERFORM | END-READ | END-RECEIVE | END-RETURN |
| END-REWRITE | END-SEARCH | END-START | END-STRING | END-SUBTRACT | END-UNSTRING | END-WRITE | ENVIRONMENT | EOP | EQUAL |
| ERROR | ESI | EVALUATE | EXCEPTION | EXIT | EXTEND | EXTERNAL | FALSE | FD | FILE |
| FILE-CONTROL | FILLER | FINAL | FIRST | FOOTING | FOR | FROM | GENERATE | GIVING | GLOBAL |
| GO | GREATER | GROUP | HEADING | HIGH-VALUE | HIGH-VALUES | I-O | I-O-CONTROL | IDENTIFICATION | IF |
| IN | INDEX | INDEXED | INDICATE | INITIAL | INITIALIZE | INITIATE | INPUT | INPUT-OUTPUT | INSPECT |
| INSTALLATION | INTO | INVALID | IS | JUST | JUSTIFIED | KEY | LABEL | LAST | LEADING |
| LEFT | LENGTH | LESS | LIMIT | LIMITS | LINAGE | LINAGE-COUNTER | LINE | LINE-COUNTER | LINES |
| LINKAGE | LOCK | LOW-VALUE | LOW-VALUES | MERGE | MESSAGE | MODE | MOVE | MULTIPLE | MULTIPLY |
| NATIVE | NEGATIVE | NEXT | NO | NOT | NUMBER | NUMERIC | NUMERIC-EDITED | OBJECT-COMPUTER | OCCURS |
| OF | OFF | OMITTED | ON | OPEN | OPTIONAL | OR | ORDER | ORGANIZATION | OTHER |
| OUTPUT | OVERFLOW | PACKED-DECIMAL | PADDING | PAGE | PAGE-COUNTER | PERFORM | PF | PH | PIC |
| PICTURE | PLUS | POINTER | POSITION | POSITIVE | PRINTING | PROCEDURE | PROCEDURES | PROCEED | PROGRAM |
| PROGRAM-ID | PURGE | QUEUE | QUOTE | QUOTES | RANDOM | RD | READ | RECEIVE | RECORD |
| RECORDS | REDEFINES | REEL | REFERENCE | REFERENCES | RELATIVE | RELEASE | REMAINDER | REMOVAL | RENAMES |
| REPLACE | REPLACING | REPORT | REPORTING | REPORTS | RESERVE | RESET | RETURN | REWIND | REWRITE |
| RF | RH | RIGHT | ROUNDED | RUN | SAME | SD | SEARCH | SECTION | SECURITY |
| SEGMENT | SEGMENT-LIMIT | SELECT | SEND | SENTENCE | SEPARATE | SEQUENCE | SEQUENTIAL | SET | SIGN |
| SIZE | SORT | SORT-MERGE | SOURCE | SOURCE-COMPUTER | SPACE | SPACES | SPECIAL-NAMES | STANDARD | STANDARD-1 |
| STANDARD-2 | START | STATUS | STOP | STRING | SUB-QUEUE-1 | SUB-QUEUE-2 | SUB-QUEUE-3 | SUBTRACT | SUM |
| SUPPRESS | SYMBOLIC | SYNC | SYNCHRONIZED | TABLE | TALLYING | TAPE | TERMINAL | TERMINATE | TEST |
| TEXT | THAN | THEN | THROUGH | THRU | TIME | TIMES | TO | TOP | TRAILING |
| TRUE | TYPE | UNIT | UNSTRING | UNTIL | UP | UPON | USAGE | USE | USING |
| VALUE | VALUES | VARYING | WHEN | WITH | WORKING-STORAGE | WRITE | ZERO | ZEROES | ZEROS |
| + | - | * | / | ** | > | < | = | >= | <= |

## List of Keywords

### PASCAL

| | | | |
|---|---|---|---|
| and | array | as | asm |
| begin | case | class | const |
| constructor | destructor | dispinterface | div |
| do | downto | else | end |
| except | exports | file | finalization |
| finally | for | function | goto |
| if | implementation | in | inherited |
| initialization | inline | interface | is |
| label | library | mod | nil |
| not | object | of | or |
| out | packed | procedure | program |
| property | raise | record | repeat |
| resourcestring | set | shl | shr |
| string | then | threadvar | to |
| try | type | unit | until |
| uses | var | while | with |

### Java

| | | | |
|---|---|---|---|
| abstract | boolean | break | byte |
| case | catch | char | class |
| const | continue | default | do |
| double | else | extends | false |
| final | finally | float | for |
| goto | if | implements | import |
| inner | instanceof | int | interface |
| long | native | new | null |
| operator | package | private | protected |
| public | return | short | static |
| strictfp | super | switch | synchronized |
| this | throw | throws | transient |
| true | try | void | volatile |
| while | | | |

## 6. Primitive Data Types

### FORTRAN

Integer Types

| type name | size (bits) | range |
|---|---|---|
| INTEGER*1 | 8 | -128 to 127 |
| INTEGER*2 | 16 | -32,768 to 32,767 |
| INTEGER or INTEGER*4 | 32 | -2,147,483,648 to 2,147,483,647 |

Floating Point Types

| type name | size (bits) | range |
|---|---|---|
| REAL or REAL*4 | 32 | -3.4E38 to 3.4E38 |
| DOUBLE PRECISION or REAL*8 | 64 | -1.7E308 to 1.7E308 |

Other Primitive Types

| type name | size (bits) | range |
|---|---|---|
| CHARACTER | 8 | Any ASCII character |
| CHARACTER*N | N*8 | |
| LOGICAL | 32 | .TRUE. or .FALSE. |

### Visual Basic

Integer Types

| type name | size (bits) | range |
|---|---|---|
| Byte | 8 | 0 to 255 |
| Integer | 16 | -32,768 to 32,767 |
| Long | 32 | -2,147,483,648 to 2,147,483,647 |

Floating Point Types

| type name | size (bits) | range |
|---|---|---|
| Single | 32 | -3.4E38 to 3.4E38 |
| Double | 64 | -1.7E308 to 1.7E308 |

Other Primitive Types

| type name | size (bits) | range |
|---|---|---|
| Currency | 64 | -922,337,203,685,477.5808 to 922,337,203,685,477.5807 |
| Boolean | 16 | True or False |
| String | 80 + string length | 0 to approximately 2 billion characters |

Visual Basic also supports Date, Variant, Object and User Defined Types

## Primitive Data Types

### C

#### Integer Types

| type name | size (bits) | minimum range |
|---|---|---|
| `int` | 16 or 32 | -32,768 to 32,767 |
| `unsigned int` | 16 to 32 | 0 to 65,535 |
| `signed int` | 16 to 32 | same as int |
| `short int` | 16 | -32,768 to 32,767 |
| `unsigned short int` | 16 | 0 to 65,535 |
| `signed short int` | 16 | same as short int |
| `long int` | 32 | -2,147,483,648 to 2,147,483,647 |
| `unsigned long int` | 32 | 0 to 4,294,967,295 |
| `signed long int` | 32 | same as long int |

Note: The size of the integer types may be system dependent.

#### Floating Point Types

| type name | size (bits) | minimum range |
|---|---|---|
| `float` | 32 | 6 digits of precision |
| `double` | 64 | 10 digits of precision |
| `long double` | 80 | 10 digits of precision |

#### Other Primitive Types

| type name | size (bits) | minimum range |
|---|---|---|
| `char` | 8 | -127 to 127 |
| `unsigned char` | 8 | 0 to 255 |
| `signed char` | 8 | -127 to 127 |

### Java

#### Integer Types

| type name | size (bits) | range |
|---|---|---|
| `byte` | 8 | -128 to 127 |
| `short` | 16 | -32,768 to 32,767 |
| `int` | 32 | -2,147,483,648 to 2,147,483,647 |
| `long` | 64 | -9,223,372,036,854,775,808 to 9,223,372,036,854,775,807 |

#### Floating Point Types

| type name | size (bits) | range |
|---|---|---|
| `float` | 32 | -3.4E38 to 3.4E38 |
| `double` | 64 | -1.7E308 to 1.7E308 |

#### Other Primitive Types

| type name | size (bits) | range |
|---|---|---|
| `char` | 16 | 0 to 65,536 |
| `boolean` | | true, false |

## Primitive Data Types

### COBOL

In Cobol the `PICTURE(PIC)` clause is used to specify the type of field, its size and its form. The two common types of field are alphanumeric and numeric.

The alphanumeric contains any character, letter, numeric digit(0-9) or special symbol.

Example:
```
05 EMPLOYEE-NAME PIC X(40)
```
An alphanumeric field of 40 bytes. The compiler will allocate 40 bytes in memory to the variable EMPLOYEE-NAME. The X character specifies an alphanumeric field and the number in the parentheses specifies the size of the field.

The numeric field contains the digits (0-9) only and optional sign.

Example:
```
05 EMPLOYEE-PAY-RATE  PIC 9(4) OR PIC 9999
```

A numeric integer field of 4 bytes. The character specifies the position of the numeric character within a field.

```
05 EMPLOYEE-TOTAL-PAY  PIC 9999V99 or PIC 9(4)V9(2).
```

A numeric field of 6 bytes. The V indicates an assumed decimal point. The V does not occupy any byte. However compiler takes a note of it. The digit after V are treated as decimal values.

All the numeric data is described as being in DISPLAY mode unless specified as COMPUTATIONAL(COMP). The use of COMP increases the program's efficiency.

Besides these Cobol has other picture clauses for data editing. They are summarized in below table

| Type of PIC clause | Description | Numeric value | Stored as |
|---|---|---|---|
| S | 02 AMT PIC S9999V99 | 156.29 | 015629^ |
|   | 02 RATE PIC V999 | 123 | 123^ |
|   | 02 BAL  PIC 9(4)V99 | -350.75 | 035075^ |
| $ | 02 AMT PIC $$999V99 | 12.49 | $1249^ |

24

## Primitive Data Types

### PASCAL

**Integer Types**

| type name | size (bits) | minimum range |
|---|---|---|
| Integer | 32 | -2,147,483,648 to 2,147,483,647 |
| Cardinal | 32 | 0 to 4,294,967,295 |
| ShortInt | 8 | -128 to 127 |
| SmallInt | 16 | -32,768 to 32,767 |
| LongInt | 32 | Same as Integer |
| Int64 | 64 | -9,223,372,036,854,775,808 to 9,223,372,036,854,775,807 |
| Byte | 8 | 0 to 255 |
| Word | 16 | 0 to 65535 |
| LongWord | 32 | 0 to 4,294,967,295 |

**Floating Point Types**

| type name | size (bits) | minimum range |
|---|---|---|
| real48 | 48 | -3.4E38 to 3.4E38 |
| Single | 32 | -3.4E38 to 3.4E38 |
| Double | 64 | -1.7E308 to 1.7E308 |
| Extended | - | -1.1E4932 to 1.1E4932 |
| Currency | 64 | -922,337,203,685,477.5808 to 922,337,203,685,477.5807 |
| Real | 64 | Same as Double |

**Other Primitive Types**

| type name | size (bits) | minimum range |
|---|---|---|
| char | 8 | -127 to 127 |
| AnsiChar | 8 | 0 to 255 |
| WideChar | 8 | -127 to 127 |
| Booelan | - | |

### Java

**Integer Types**

| type name | size (bits) | range |
|---|---|---|
| byte | 8 | -128 to 127 |
| short | 16 | -32,768 to 32,767 |
| int | 32 | -2,147,483,648 to 2,147,483,647 |
| long | 64 | -9,223,372,036,854,775,808 to 9,223,372,036,854,775,807 |

**Floating Point Types**

| type name | size (bits) | range |
|---|---|---|
| float | 32 | -3.4E38 to 3.4E38 |
| double | 64 | -1.7E308 to 1.7E308 |

**Other Primitive Types**

| type name | size (bits) | range |
|---|---|---|
| char | 16 | 0 to 65,536 |
| boolean | | true, false |

## 7. Declaring and Initializing Variables

| FORTRAN | Visual Basic |
|---|---|
| Syntax for declaring a variable:<br><br>`type name`<br><br>where<br>    `type` is the name of the type<br>    `name` is the name of the variable<br><br>Examples:<br><br>`Integer x, y`<br>`Double Precision a`<br><br>Variables cannot be initialized at time they are declared. Variables can be initialized in the code as follows:<br><br>`x= 45`<br>`a = 36.3`<br>`b = 45.7`<br><br>Note:<br>Any uninitialized variables automatically get set to zero if numeric type.<br><br>Variables must be declared before any executable statements. | Syntax for declaring a variable:<br><br>`Dim  name as type`<br><br>where<br>    `Dim` and `As` are visual basic keywords<br>    `type` is the name of the type<br>    `name` is the name of the variable<br><br>Examples:<br><br>`Dim x as Integer, y as Integer`<br>`Dim a as Double, b as Double`<br><br>Variables cannot be initialized at time they are declared. Variables can be initialized in the code as follows:<br><br>`x= 45`<br>`a = 36.3: b = 45.7`<br><br>Note:<br>Any uninitialized variables automatically get set to zero if numeric type, or to Nothing if reference type.<br><br>Public or Private keywords can also be used to declare variables to control their visibility.<br><br>Variables can be declared anywhere within a procedure, before they are used. It is a good practice to declare all the variables at the top of a procedure. |

## Declaring and Initializing Variables

| C | Java |
|---|---|
| Syntax for declaring a variable:<br><br>`type name`<br><br>where<br><br>    `type` is the name of the type<br>    `name` is the name of the variable<br><br>Examples:<br><br>`int x, y, z;`<br>`double a;`<br><br>Variables can also be initialized at the time they are declared.<br><br>`int x= 45;`<br>`double a = 36.3, b = 45.7;`<br><br>Variables declared within functions (local variables), if uninitialized, will have unknown values. Global and static variables, if uninitialized, will be set to zero.<br><br>In C, variables must be declared before any executable statements. | Syntax for declaring a variable:<br><br>`type name`<br><br>where<br><br>    `type` is the name of the type<br>    `name` is the name of the variable<br><br>Examples:<br><br>`int x, y, z;`<br>`double a;`<br><br>Variables can also be initialized at the time they are declared<br><br>`int x= 45;`<br>`double a = 36.3, b = 45.7;`<br><br>A variable declared at the class level and not explicitly initialized, automatically gets initialized to zero if numeric type, or to null if reference type.<br>A variable declared within a method must be initialized before it can be used.<br>Variables can be declared anywhere within a procedure, before they are used. It is a good practice to declare all the variables at the top of a procedure. |

### Declaring and Initializing Variables

## COBOL

The alphanumeric contains any character, letter, numeric digit(0-9) or special symbol.

Example:
```
  05 EMPLOYEE-NAME PIC X(40)
```
An alphanumeric field of 40 bytes. The compiler will allocate 40 bytes in memory to the variable EMPLOYEE-NAME. The X character specifies an alphanumeric field and the number in the parentheses specifies the size of the field.

The numeric field contains the digits (0-9) only and optional sign.

Example:

```
  05 EMPLOYEE-PAY-RATE   PIC 9(4) OR PIC 9999
```

A numeric integer field of 4 bytes. The character specifies the position of the numeric character within a field.

```
  05 EMPLOYEE-TOTAL-PAY   PIC 9999V99 or PIC 9(4)V9(2).
```

A numeric field of 6 bytes. The V indicates an assumed decimal point. The V does not occupy any byte. However the compiler takes note of it. The digits after V are treated as decimal values.

## Declaring and Initializing Variables

| PASCAL | Java |
|---|---|
| Declaring and initializing variables:<br><br>Syntax for declaring a variable<br><br>`name : type`<br><br>where<br>    `type` is the name of the type<br>    `name` is the name of the variable<br><br>Examples:<br><br>`x, y, z   : Integer;`<br>`a         : double;`<br><br>Variables can also be initialized at the time they are declared.<br><br>`x : Integer = 45;`<br>`a : double = 36.3;`<br>`b : double = 45.7;`<br><br>Variables are not initialized ever, unless a class constructor specifically initializes it. Therefore, variables must always be initialized before they are used. | Syntax for declaring a variable:<br><br>`type name`<br><br>where<br><br>    `type` is the name of the type<br>    `name` is the name of the variable<br><br>Examples:<br><br>`int x, y, z;`<br>`double a;`<br><br>Variables can also be initialized at the time they are declared<br><br>`int x= 45;`<br>`double a = 36.3, b = 45.7;`<br><br>A variable declared at the class level and not explicitly initialized, automatically gets initialized to zero if numeric type, or to null if reference type.<br>A variable declared within a method must be initialized before it can be used.<br>Variables can be declared anywhere within a procedure, before they are used. It is a good practice to declare all the variables at the top of a procedure. |

## 8. Operators – Arithmetic

### FORTRAN

| Description | Operator | Example (Integer a, b) |
|---|---|---|
| Addition | + | y = a + b |
| Subtraction | - | y = a - b |
| Multiplication | * | y = a * b |
| Division | / | y = a / b |
| Modulus | Mod function | y = Mod(a,b) |
| Exponentiation | ** | y = a ** b |
| Simple Assignment | = | y = a |

### Visual Basic

| Description | Operator | Example (Dim a as integer, b as integer) |
|---|---|---|
| Addition | + | y = a + b |
| Subtraction | - | y = a - b |
| Multiplication | * | y = a * b |
| Division | / | y = a / b |
| Modulus | Mod | y = a Mod b |
| Integer Division | \ | y = a \ b |
| Exponentiation | ^ | y = a ^ b |
| Simple Assignment | = | y = a |

**Operators – Arithmetic**

## C

| Description | Operator | Example (int a=41, b=1) |
|---|---|---|
| Addition | + | y = a + b; |
| Subtraction | - | y = a - b; |
| Multiplication | * | y = a * b; |
| Division | / | y = a / b; |
| Modulus | % | y = a % b; |
| Addition Assignment | += | y += a; |
| Simple Assignment | = | y = a; |
| Subtraction Assignment | -= | y -= a; |
| Multiplication Assignment | *= | y *= a; |
| Division Assignment | /= | y /= a; |
| Modulus Assignment | %= | y %=a; |
| Increment | ++ | y = ++a; |
| Decrement | -- | y = --b; |
| Exponentiation | pow() | pow(a,b) |

## Java

| Description | Operator | Example (int a=41, b=1) |
|---|---|---|
| Addition | + | y = a + b; |
| Subtraction | - | y = a - b; |
| Multiplication | * | y = a * b; |
| Division | / | y = a / b; |
| Modulus | % | y = a % b; |
| Addition Assignment | += | y += a; |
| Simple Assignment | = | y = a; |
| Subtraction Assignment | -= | y -= a; |
| Multiplication Assignment | *= | y *= a; |
| Division Assignment | /= | y /= a; |
| Modulus Assignment | /% | y %=a; |
| Increment | ++ | y = ++a; |
| Decrement | -- | y = --b; |
| Exponentiation | Math.pow() | Math.pow(a,b) |

**Operators – Arithmetic**

## COBOL

| Description | Verb | Example (a = 41, b = 1) |
|---|---|---|
| Addition | ADD | ADD A TO B |
| Subtraction | SUBTRACT | SUBTRACT A FROM B |
| Multiplication | MULTIPLY | MULTIPLY A BY B |
| Division | DIVIDE | DIVIDE A INTO B |
| Modulus | % | A % B |
| Simple Assignment | MOVE | MOVE A TO Y |
| Exponentiation | ** | A ** B |

## Operators – Arithmetic

### PASCAL

| Description | Operator | Example (a : Integer= 41; b : Integer= 1) |
|---|---|---|
| Addition | + | y := a + b; |
| Subtraction | - | y := a - b; |
| Multiplication | * | y := a * b; |
| Division | / | y := a / b; |
| Modulus | % | y := a % b; |
| Integer division | div | y := a div b; |
| Simple Assignment | := | y:= a; |
| Increment | Inc() | Inc(a); |
| Decrement | Dec() | Dec(a); |
| Exponentiation | power() | power(a,b); |

### Java

| Description | Operator | Example (int a=41, b=1) |
|---|---|---|
| Addition | + | y = a + b; |
| Subtraction | - | y = a - b; |
| Multiplication | * | y = a * b; |
| Division | / | y = a / b; |
| Modulus | % | y = a % b; |
| Addition Assignment | += | y += a; |
| Simple Assignment | = | y = a; |
| Subtraction Assignment | -= | y -= a; |
| Multiplication Assignment | *= | y *= a; |
| Division Assignment | /= | y /= a; |
| Modulus Assignment | /% | y %=a; |
| Increment | ++ | y = ++a; |
| Decrement | -- | y = --b; |
| Exponentiation | Math.pow() | Math.pow(a,b) |

33

## 9. Operators – Relational

### FORTRAN

| Description | Operator | Examples (integer a,b a=5, b=10 logical d) |
|---|---|---|
| Equal to | .EQ. | d = (a.EQ.b) |
| Not equal to | .NE. | d = (a.NE.b) |
| Greater than | .GT. | d = (a .GT. b) |
| Less than | .LT. | d = (a .LT. b) |
| Greater than or equal to | .GE. | d = (a .GE. b) |
| Less than or equal to | .LE. | d = (a .LE. b) |

### Visual Basic

| Description | Operator | Examples (Integer a,b a=5, b=10 Boolean d) |
|---|---|---|
| Equal to | = | d = (a = b) |
| Not equal to | <> | d = (a <> b) |
| Greater than | > | d = (a > b) |
| Less than | < | d = (a < b) |
| Greater than or equal to | >= | d = (a >= b) |
| Less than or equal to | <= | d = (a <= b) |

## Operators – Relational

### C

| Description | Operator | Examples (int a=5, b=10; int d;) |
|---|---|---|
| Equal to | == | d = (a==b);<br>// d will be 0 |
| Not equal to | != | d = (a!=b);<br>// d will be 1 |
| Greater than | > | d = (a > b);<br>// d will be 0 |
| Less than | < | d = (a < b);<br>// d will be 1 |
| Greater than or equal to | >= | d = (a >= b);<br>// d will be 1 |
| Less than or equal to | <= | d = (a <= b);<br>// d will be 0 |

### Java

| Description | Operator | Examples (int a=5, b=10; boolean d;) |
|---|---|---|
| Equal to | == | d = (a==b);<br>// d will be false |
| Not equal to | != | d = (a!=b);<br>// d will be true |
| Greater than | > | d = (a > b);<br>// d will be false |
| Less than | < | d = (a < b);<br>// d will be true |
| Greater than or equal to | >= | d = (a >= b);<br>// d will be true |
| Less than or equal to | <= | d = (a <= b);<br>// d will be false |

**Operators – Relational**

## COBOL

| Description | Operator |
|---|---|
| Equal to | `=` or `IS EQUAL TO` |
| Not equal to | `NOT=` or `IS NOT EQUAL TO` or `<>` |
| Greater than | `>` or `IS GREATER THAN` |
| Less than | `<` or `IS LESS THAN` |
| Not greater than | `NOT >` or `IS NOT GREATER THAN` |
| Not less than | `NOT <` or `IS NO LESS THAN` |

## Operators – Relational

### PASCAL

| Description | Operator | Examples<br>(a: Integer=5;<br>b: Integer=10;<br>d:Boolean;) |
|---|---|---|
| Equal to | = | `d = (a = b);` |
| Not equal to | <> | `d = (a <> b);` |
| Greater than | > | `d = (a > b);` |
| Less than | < | `d = (a < b);` |
| Greater than or equal to | >= | `d = (a >= b);` |
| Less than or equal to | <= | `d = (a <= b);` |

### Java

| Description | Operator | Examples<br>(int a=5, b=10;<br>boolean d;) |
|---|---|---|
| Equal to | == | `d = (a==b);`<br>`// d will be false` |
| Not equal to | != | `d = (a!=b);`<br>`// d will be true` |
| Greater than | > | `d = (a > b);`<br>`// d will be false` |
| Less than | < | `d = (a < b);`<br>`// d will be true` |
| Greater than or equal to | >= | `d = (a >= b);`<br>`// d will be true` |
| Less than or equal to | <= | `d = (a <= b);`<br>`// d will be false` |

## 10. Operators – Bitwise and Boolean

### FORTRAN

**Bitwise Operators**

Certain versions of Fortran may contain functions for bit-manipulation of integers. These functions are not commonly used in Fortran.

**Boolean Operators**

| Description | Operator |
|---|---|
| Logical AND | .AND. |
| Logical OR | .OR. |
| Logical XOR | .XOR. |
| Logical NOT | .NOT. |
| Equivalence | .EQV. |
| Nonequivalence | .NEQV. |

### Visual Basic

**Bitwise Operators**

| Description | Operator |
|---|---|
| Logical AND | AND |
| Logical OR | OR |
| Logical XOR | XOR |
| Logical NOT | NOT |
| Logical Equivalence | Eqv |
| Logical Implication | Imp |

**Boolean Operators**

| Description | Operator |
|---|---|
| Logical AND | AND |
| Logical OR | OR |
| Logical XOR | XOR |
| Logical NOT | NOT |
| Logical Equivalence | Eqv |
| Logical Implication | Imp |

# Operators – Bitwise and Boolean

## C

### Bitwise Operators

| Description | Operator |
|---|---|
| Bitwise unary NOT | ~ |
| Bitwise AND | & |
| Bitwise OR | \| |
| Shift right | >> |
| Shift left | << |
| Bitwise AND assignment | &= |
| Bitwise OR assignment | \|= |
| Shift right assignment | >>= |
| Shift left assignment | <<= |

### Boolean Operators

| Description | Operator |
|---|---|
| Logical AND | && |
| Logical OR | \|\| |
| Logical unary NOT | ! |
| AND assignment | &= |
| OR assignment | \|= |
| Equal to | == |
| Not equal to | != |

## Java

### Bitwise Operators

| Description | Operator |
|---|---|
| Bitwise unary NOT | ~ |
| Bitwise AND | & |
| Bitwise OR | \| |
| Bitwise exclusive OR | ^ |
| Shift right | >> |
| Shift right zero fill | >>> |
| Shift left | << |
| Bitwise AND assignment | &= |
| Bitwise OR assignment | \|= |
| Bitwise exclusive OR assignment | ^= |
| Shift right assignment | >>= |
| Shift right zero fill assignment | >>>= |
| Shift left assignment | <<= |

### Boolean Operators

| Description | Operator |
|---|---|
| Logical AND | & |
| Logical OR | \| |
| Logical XOR | ^ |
| Short-circuit OR | \|\| |
| Short-circuit AND | && |
| Logical unary NOT | ! |
| AND assignment | &= |
| OR assignment | \|= |
| XOR assignment | ^= |
| Equal to | == |
| Not equal to | != |

## Operators – Bitwise and Boolean

### COBOL

**Boolean Operators**

| Description | Operator |
|---|---|
| Logical AND | AND |
| Logical OR | OR |
| Logical NOT | NOT |
| Equivalence | = or EQUAL TO |
| Non-Equivalence | NOT or <> |

Cobol does not have bitwise operators.

## Operators – Bitwise and Boolean

### PASCAL

**Bitwise Operators**

| Description | Operator |
|---|---|
| Bitwise AND | `and` |
| Bitwise OR | `or` |
| Bitwise XOR | `xor` |
| Bitwise NOT | `not` |
| Bitwise shift left | `shl` |
| Bitwise shift right | `shr` |

**Boolean Operators**

| Description | Operator |
|---|---|
| Logical AND | `and` |
| Logical OR | `or` |
| Logical XOR | `xor` |
| Logical NOT | `not` |
| Equality | `=` |

### Java

**Bitwise Operators**

| Description | Operator |
|---|---|
| Bitwise unary NOT | ~ |
| Bitwise AND | & |
| Bitwise OR | \| |
| Bitwise exclusive OR | ^ |
| Shift right | >> |
| Shift right zero fill | >>> |
| Shift left | << |
| Bitwise AND assignment | &= |
| Bitwise OR assignment | \|= |
| Bitwise exclusive OR assignment | ^= |
| Shift right assignment | >>= |
| Shift right zero fill assignment | >>>= |
| Shift left assignment | <<= |

**Boolean Operators**

| Description | Operator |
|---|---|
| Logical AND | & |
| Logical OR | \| |
| Logical XOR | ^ |
| Short-circuit OR | \|\| |
| Short-circuit AND | && |
| Logical unary NOT | ! |
| AND assignment | &= |
| OR assignment | \|= |
| XOR assignment | ^= |
| Equal to | == |
| Not equal to | != |

## 11. Operator Precedence

| FORTRAN | Visual Basic |
|---|---|
| ( ) | ( ) |
| ** | ^ |
| - (Unary negation) | - (Unary negation) |
| *   / | *   / |
| Mod | \ |
| +   - | Mod |
| .EQ.  .NE.  .LE.  .GE.  .LT.  .GT. | +   - |
| .NOT. | & |
| .AND. | =   <>   <=   >=   >   < |
| .OR. | Not |
| .XOR. | And |
| .EQV. | Or |
| .NEQV. | Xor |
|  | Eqv |
|  | Imp |

**Operator Precedence**

| C | Java |
|---|---|
| `()   [ ]   ->   .`           <br> `!   ~   ++   --   (type)   *   &   sizeof` <br> `*   /   %` <br> `+   -` <br> `>>   <<` <br> `>   >=   <   <=` <br> `==   !=` <br> `&` <br> `^` <br> `\|` <br> `&&` <br> `\|\|` <br> `?:` <br> `=   +=   -=   *=   /=` | `()   [ ]   .` <br> `++   --   ~   !` <br> `*   /   %` <br> `+   -` <br> `>>   >>>   <<` <br> `>   >=   <   <=` <br> `==   !=` <br> `&` <br> `^` <br> `\|` <br> `&&` <br> `\|\|` <br> `?:` <br> `=   +=   -=   *=   /=` |

**Operator Precedence**

| COBOL |
|---|
| ( ) |
| ** |
| *   / |
| Mod |
| +   − |
| =   <>   >   <   NOT>   NOT< |

## Operator Precedence

| PASCAL | Java |
|---|---|
| `()    not` | `()    [ ]    .` |
| `*    /` | `++    --    ~    !` |
| `div  mod  as   and  shl  shr` | `*    /    %` |
| `+    -` | `+    -` |
| `or   xor` | `>>    >>>    <<` |
| `=    <>    <=    >=    >    <` | `>    >=    <    <=` |
| `in   is` | `==    !=` |
| | `&` |
| | `^` |
| | `\|` |
| | `&&` |
| | `\|\|` |
| | `?:` |
| | `=    +=    -=    *=    /=` |

## 12. Decision Making with *if* Statement

| FORTRAN | Visual Basic |
|---|---|
| *if (condition) statement1*<br><br>or<br><br>*if (condition) then*<br>   *statement1*<br>   *statement2*<br>     ⋮<br>     ⋮<br><br>*endif*<br><br><br>*condition* is any statement that returns a boolean value. | *If condition Then statement1*<br><br>or<br><br>*If condition then*<br>   *statement1*<br>   *statement2*<br>     ⋮<br>     ⋮<br><br>*End If*<br><br><br>*condition* is any statement that returns a boolean value. |
| ```
INTEGER*4 X,Y,Z
X =3
Y =4
Z =0

    IF (X.LT.Y) Z = 99
OR

    IF (X.LT.Y) THEN
        Z=99
        :
    END IF
``` | ```
Dim x as Integer, y as Integer, z as Integer
x =3
y =4
z =0

    If x < y Then z = 99

or

    If x < y Then
        z=99
        :
    End If
``` |

## Decision Making with *if* Statement

| C | Java |
|---|---|
| *if (condition) statement1;*<br><br>or<br><br>*if (condition)*<br>*{*<br>   *statement1;*<br>   *statement2;*<br>     :<br>     :<br>*}*<br><br>Each statement may be a single statement or compound statement enclosed in curly braces.<br><br>*condition* can be any expression that evaluates to true (non-zero) or false (zero). | *if (condition) statement1;*<br><br>or<br><br>*if (condition) {*<br>   *statement1;*<br>   *statement2;*<br>     :<br>     :<br>*}*<br><br>Each statement may be a single statement or compound statement enclosed in curly braces.<br><br>*condition* is any statement that returns a boolean value. |
| ```
int x=3, y=4, Z=0;

if (x < y) z=99;

or
    if (x < y)
    {
       z = 99;
         :
         :
    }
``` | ```
int x=3, y=4, Z=0;

if (x < y) z=99;

or

    if (x < y) {
       z = 99;
         :
         :
    }
``` |

## Decision Making with *if* Statement

### COBOL

*if condition statement1.*

or

*if condition*
   *statement1*
   *statement2*
     :
     :
   *statementn.*

Each statement may be a single statement or multiple statements terminated by (.).

*condition* can be any expression that evaluates to `true` or `false`.

---

X = 3, Y = 4, Z = 0

```
IF X < Y MOVE 99 TO Z.
```

or

```
    IF X < Y

        MOVE 99 TO Z
          :
          :
        MOVE 99 TO X.
```

## Decision Making with *if* Statement

| PASCAL | Java |
|---|---|
| `if (condition) Then statement1`<br><br>or<br><br>`if (condition) then`<br>`begin`<br>`   statement1`<br>`   statement2`<br>`      :`<br>`      :`<br>`end;`<br><br><br>*condition* is any statement that returns a boolean value. | `if (condition) statement1;`<br><br>or<br><br>`if (condition) {`<br>`   statement1;`<br>`   statement2;`<br>`      :`<br>`      :`<br>`}`<br><br>Each statement may be a single statement or compound statement enclosed in curly braces.<br><br>*condition* is any statement that returns a boolean value. |
| `x, y, z  :Integer;`<br>`x := 3;`<br>`y := 4;`<br>`Z := 0;`<br><br>`if (x < y) Then z:=99;`<br><br>or<br><br>`    if (x < y) Then`<br>`    begin`<br>`       z := 99;`<br>`          :`<br>`          :`<br>`    end;` | `int x=3, y=4, Z=0;`<br><br>`if (x < y) z=99;`<br><br>or<br><br>`    if (x < y) {`<br>`       z = 99;`<br>`          :`<br>`          :`<br>`    }` |

## 13. Decision Making with *if . . . else* Statement

| FORTRAN | Visual Basic |
|---|---|
| `if (condition) then`<br>`    statement1`<br>`    statement2`<br>`    :`<br>`else`<br>`    statement3`<br>`    statement4`<br>`    :`<br>`endif` | `If condition Then`<br>`    statement1`<br>`    statement2`<br>`    :`<br>`Else`<br>`    statement3`<br>`    statement4`<br>`    :`<br>`End If` |
| `Integer*4 x,y,z`<br>`x =3`<br>`y =4`<br>`z =0`<br><br>`    if (x.LT.y) then`<br>`        z=99`<br>`        :`<br>`    else`<br>`        z=98`<br>`        :`<br>`    end if` | `Dim x as Integer, y as Integer, z as Integer`<br>`x =3`<br>`y =4`<br>`z =0`<br><br>`    If x < y Then`<br>`        z=99`<br>`        :`<br>`    Else`<br>`        z=98`<br>`        :`<br>`    End If` |

## Decision Making with *if...else* Statement

| C | Java |
|---|---|
| `if (condition) statement1;`<br>`else statement2;`<br><br>or<br><br>`if (condition)`<br>`{`<br>`   statement1;`<br>`   statement2;`<br>`      :`<br>`} else`<br>`{`<br>`   statement3;`<br>`   statement4;`<br>`      :`<br>`}` | `if (condition) statement1;`<br>`else statement2;`<br><br>or<br><br>`if (condition) {`<br>`   statement1;`<br>`   statement2;`<br>`      :`<br>`} else {`<br>`   statement3;`<br>`   statement4;`<br>`      :`<br>`}` |
| `int x=3, y=4, Z=0;`<br>`    if (x < y) z=99;`<br>`    else z=98;`<br>`or`<br>`    if (x < y)`<br>`    {`<br>`       z = 99;`<br>`         :`<br>`         :`<br>`    } else`<br>`    {`<br>`       z = 98;`<br>`         :`<br>`    }` | `int x=3, y=4, Z=0;`<br>`    if (x < y) z=99;`<br>`    else z=98;`<br>`or`<br><br>`    if (x < y) {`<br>`       z = 99;`<br>`         :`<br>`         :`<br>`    }else {`<br>`       z = 98;`<br>`         :`<br>`    }` |

## Decision Making with *if...else* Statement

### COBOL

```
IF CONDITION
    STATEMENT1
    STATEMENT2
    :

ELSE
     STATEMENT3
     STATEMENT4
    :
END-IF
```

```
X = 3
Y = 4
Z = 0


    IF X < Y
        MOVE 99 TO Z
         :
    ELSE
        MOVE 98 TO Z
         :
    END-IF.
```

## Decision Making with *if...else* Statement

| PASCAL | Java |
|---|---|
| ```
if (condition) then
   begin
      statement1;
      statement2;
      :
   end
else
   begin
      statement3;
      statement4;
      :
end;
``` | ```
if (condition) statement1;
else statement2;
```           or
```
if (condition) {
   statement1;
   statement2;
   :
} else {
   statement3;
   statement4;
   :
}
``` |
| ```
x, y, z : Integer;
x := 3;   y := 4;   z := 0;
if (x<y) then
  z := 99
 else
  z := 98;
```            or
```
if (x<y) then
   begin
      z := 99;
      :
      :
   end
else
   begin
      z := 98;
      :
end;
``` | ```
int x=3, y=4, Z=0;
   if (x < y) z=99;
   else z=98;
```            or
```
   if (x < y) {
      z = 99;
      :
      :
   }else {
      z = 98;
      :
   }
``` |

53

## 14. Decision Making with *if ... elseif ... else* Statement

| FORTRAN | Visual Basic |
|---|---|
| ```
if (condition1) then
    statement1
    statement2
    :
elseif(condition2) then
    statement3
    statement4
    :
elseif(condition3) then
    statement5
    statement6
    :
else
    statement7
    statement8
    :
endif
``` | ```
If condition1 Then
    statement1
    statement2
    :
Else If condition2 Then
    statement3
    statement4
    :
Else If condition3 Then
    statement5
    statement6
    :
Else
    statement7
    statement8
    :
End If
``` |

## Decision Making with *if ... elseif ... else* Statement

| C | Java |
|---|---|
| ```
if (condition1) statement1;
else if(condition2) statement2;
else if(condition2) statement3;
else statement4;

or

if (condition1)
{
   statement1;
   statement2;
      :
}
else if(condition2)
{
   statement3;
   statement4;
      :
}
else if(condition3)
{
   statement5;
   statement6;
      :
}
else
{
   statement7;
   statement8;
      :
}
``` | ```
if (condition1) statement1;
else if(condition2) statement2;
else if(condition2) statement3;
else statement4;

or

if (condition1) {
   statement1;
   statement2;
      :
} else if(condition2) {
   statement3;
   statement4;
      :
} else if(condition3) {
   statement5;
   statement6;
      :
}else {
   statement7;
   statement8;
      :
}
``` |

## Decision Making with *if … elseif … else* Statement

### COBOL

```
IF CONDITION1
    STATEMENT1
    STATEMENT2
    :
ELSE
    IF CONDITION2
       STATEMENT3
       STATEMENT4
    :
ELSE
    IF CONDITION3
       STATEMENT5
       STATEMENT6
         :
ELSE
       STATEMENT7
       STATEMENT8
    :
END-IF.
```

## Decision Making with *if … elseif … else* Statement

| PASCAL | Java |
|---|---|
| <pre>if (condition1) then statement1;
else if (condition2) then statement2;
else if (condition3) then statement3;
else statement4;


if (condition1) then
   begin
      statement1;
      statement2;
      :
   end
else if (condition2) then
   begin
      statement3;
      statement4;
      :
   end
else if (condition3) then
   begin
      statement5;
      statement6;
      :
   end
else
   begin
      statement7;
      statement8;
      :
end;</pre> | <pre>if (condition1) statement1;
else if(condition2) statement2;
else if(condition2) statement3;
else statement4;

 or

if (condition1) {
   statement1;
   statement2;
   :
} else if(condition2) {
   statement3;
   statement4;
   :
} else if(condition3) {
   statement5;
   statement6;
   :
}else {
   statement7;
   statement8;
   :
}</pre> |

## 15. Decision Making with *if ... elseif ... else* Statement – Example

| FORTRAN | Visual Basic |
|---|---|
| ```
IF (SCORE .GT. 90) THEN
    GRADE = 'A'
    X=95.0

ELSE IF (SCORE .GT. 80)   THEN
    GRADE = 'B'
    X=85.0

ELSE IF (SCORE .GT. 70)   THEN
    GRADE = 'C'
    X=75.0

ELSE
    GRADE = 'F'
    X=65.0
ENDIF
``` | ```
If score > 90 Then
    grade = "A"
    x=95.0

Else If score > 80   Then
    grade = "B"
    x=85.0

Else If score > 70   Then
    grade = "C"
    x=75.0

Else
    grade = "F"
    x=65.0
End If
``` |

## Decision Making with *if … elseif … else* Statement – Example

| C | Java |
|---|---|
| ```
if (score > 90) grade = 'A';
else if (score > 80) grade = 'B';
else if (score > 70) grade = 'C';
else grade = 'F';

or

if (score > 90)
{
    grade = 'A';
    x=95.0;
}
else if (score > 80)
{
    grade = 'B';
    x=85.0;
}
else if (score > 70)
{
    grade = 'C';
    x=75.0;
}
else
{
    grade = 'F';
    x=65.0;
}
``` | ```
if (score > 90) grade = 'A';
else if (score > 80) grade = 'B';
else if (score > 70) grade = 'C';
else grade = 'F';

or

if (score > 90) {
    grade = 'A';
    x=95.0;
}
else if (score > 80) {
    grade = 'B';
    x=85.0;
}
else if (score > 70) {
    grade = 'C';
    x=75.0;
}
else{
    grade = 'F';
    x=65.0;
}
``` |

**Decision Making with *if ... elseif ... else* Statement -- Example**

## COBOL

```
IF SCORE > 90
    MOVE "A" TO GRADE
    MOVE 95 TO X
ELSE
    IF SCORE > 80
    MOVE "B" TO GRADE
    MOVE 85 TO X
ELSE
    IF SCORE > 70
    MOVE "C" TO GRADE
    MOVE 75 TO X
ELSE
    MOVE "F" TO GRADE
    MOVE 65 TO X
END-IF.
```

## Decision Making with *if ... elseif ... else* Statement -- Example

| PASCAL | Java |
|---|---|
| ```pascal
if (score > 90) then grade := 'A'
else if (score > 80) then grade := 'B'
else if (score > 70) then grade := 'C'
else grade := 'F';


if (score > 90) then
begin
   grade := 'A';
   x := 95.0;
end
else if (score > 80) then
begin
   grade := 'B';
   x := 85.0;
end
else if (score > 70) then
begin
   grade := 'C';
   x := 75.0;
end
else
begin
   grade := 'F';
   x := 65.0;
end;
``` | ```java
if (score > 90) grade = 'A';
else if (score > 80) grade = 'B';
else if (score > 70) grade = 'C';
else grade = 'F';

or

if (score > 90) {
     grade = 'A';
     x=95.0;
}
else if (score > 80) {
     grade = 'B';
     x=85.0;
}
else if (score > 70) {
     grade = 'C';
     x=75.0;
}
else{
     grade = 'F';
     x=65.0;
}
``` |

## 16. Decision Making with *switch*, *Select Case*, *Evaluate* or *case () of* Statements

| FORTRAN | Visual Basic |
|---|---|
| `Select Case (expression)`<br>`case (val1)`<br>   `statement1`<br>   `statement2`<br><br>`case (val2)`<br>   `statement3`<br>   `statement4`<br>     :<br>     :<br>     :<br>`case (valn)`<br>   `statement11`<br>   `statement21`<br><br><br>`case default`<br>   `statement31`<br>   `statement41`<br>`End Select`<br><br>The *expression* must be of type `INTEGER`, `LOGICAL` or `CHARACTER*1`.<br>Case values must be constants or literals.<br>Duplicate or overlapping case values are not allowed. | `Select Case expression`<br>`case val1`<br>   `statement1`<br>   `statement2`<br><br>`case val2`<br>   `statement3`<br>   `statement4`<br>     :<br>     :<br>     :<br>`case valn`<br>   `statement11`<br>   `statement21`<br><br><br>`case else`<br>   `statement31`<br>   `statement41`<br>`End Select`<br><br>The *expression* may be of any type. Case values must be constants or literals.<br>It does not check for duplicate or overlapping case values. |

**Decision Making with *switch*, *Select Case*, *Evaluate* or *case() of* Statements**

| C | Java |
|---|---|
| ```
switch (expression)
{
case val1:
   statement1;
   statement2;
   break;

case val2:
   statement3;
   statement4;
   :
   :
   :
break;
case valn:
   statement11;
   statement21;
   break;

default:
   statement31;
   statement41;
}
```<br><br>The *expression* must be of the type `integer` or *character*.<br>The case values must be constants or literals.<br>Duplicate case values are not allowed. | ```
switch (expression){
case val1:
   statement1;
   statement2;
   break;

case val2:
   statement3;
   statement4;

   :
   :
   :
   break;
case valn:
   statement11;
   statement21;
   break;

default:
   statement31;
   statement41;
}
```<br><br>The *expression* must be of the type `int`, `byte`, `short` or `char`.<br>The case values must be constants or literals.<br>Duplicate case values are not allowed. |

## Decision Making with *switch*, *Select Case*, *Evaluate* or *case() of* Statements

### COBOL

```
EVALUATE VARIABLE
WHEN CASE-1
    STATEMENT1
    STATEMENT2
    :
WHEN CASE-2
    STATEMENT1
    STATEMENT2
    :
WHEN CASE-N
    STATEMENT1
    STATEMENT2
    :
WHEN OTHER
    STATEMENT1
    STATEMENT2
    :
END-EVALUATE.
```

## Decision Making with *switch, Select Case, Evaluate* or *case() of* Statements

| PASCAL | Java |
|---|---|
| ```
case (expression) of
  val1: begin
          statement1;
          statement2;
        end;
  val2: begin
          statement3;
          statement4;
            :
            :
            :
        end;
  valn: begin
          statement11;
          statement21;
        end;
  else
    begin
      statement31;
      statement41;
    end;
end
``` | ```
switch (expression){
case val1:
    statement1;
    statement2;
    break;

case val2:
    statement3;
    statement4;
      :
      :
      :
    break;
case valn:
    statement11;
    statement21;
    break;

default:
    statement31;
    statement41;
}
``` |
| The expression must be an ordinal type. The case values cannot overlap and must be either literals or constants. | The *expression* must be of the type int, byte, short or char. The case values must be constants or literals. Duplicate case values are not allowed. |

65

## 17. Decision Making with *switch*, *Select Case*, *Evaluate* or *case() of* Statements – Example 1

| FORTRAN | Visual Basic |
|---|---|
| <pre>Select Case (M)
   Case (1)
     Month = 'January'
     Season = 'winter'
   Case (4)
     Month = 'April'
     Season = 'Spring'
   Case (7)
     Month = 'July'
     Season = 'Summer'
   Case (10)
     Month = 'October'
     Season = 'Fall'
   Case Default
     Month = 'Not beginning'//
  &        ' of a quarter'
     Season = 'Undefined'
End Select</pre> | <pre>Select Case M
Case 1
    Month = "January"
    Season = "winter"
Case 4
    Month = "April"
    Season = "Spring"
Case 7
    Month = "July"
    Season = "Summer"
Case 10
    Month = "October"
    Season = "Fall"
Case Else
    Month = "Not beginning of a quarter"
    Season = "Undefined"
End Select</pre> |

## Decision Making with *switch*, *Select Case*, *Evaluate* or *case() of* Statements – Example 1

| C | Java |
|---|---|
| ```
switch (n)
{
case 1:    strcpy(month, "January");
           strcpy(season, "winter");
           break;
case 4:    strcpy(month, "April");
           strcpy(season, "Spring");
           break;
case 7:    strcpy(month, "July");
           strcpy(season, "Summer");
           break;
case 10:   strcpy(month, "October");
           strcpy(season, "Fall");
           break;
default:   strcpy(month,
           "Not beginning of a quarter");
           strcpy(season, "undefined");
}
``` | ```
switch (n) {
case 1:    month="January";
           season="winter";
           break;
case 4:    month="April";
           season="Spring";
           break;
case 7:    month="July";
           season="Summer";
           break;
case 10:   month="October";
           season="Fall";
           break;
default:   month="Not beginning"+
               "of a quarter";
           season="undefined";
}
``` |

## Decision Making with *switch*, *Select Case*, *Evaluate* or *case() of* Statements – Example 1

### COBOL

```
EVALUATE N
WHEN 1
      MOVE "January" TO MONTH
      MOVE "winter" TO SEASON
WHEN 4
      MOVE  "April" TO MONTH
      MOVE "Spring" TO SEASON
WHEN 7
      MOVE "July" TO MONTH
       MOVE "Summer" TO SEASON
WHEN 10
      MOVE "October" TO MONTH
       MOVE "Fall" TO SEASON
WHEN OTHER
 MOVE "Not beginning of a quarter" TO MONTH
        MOVE "undefined" TO SEASON
END-EVALUATE.
```

## Decision Making with *switch*, *Select Case*, *Evaluate* or *case() of* Statements – Example 1

| PASCAL | Java |
|---|---|
| <pre>case n of
  1: begin
       month  := 'January';
       season := 'winter';
     end;
  4: begin
       month  := 'April';
       season := 'Spring';
     end;
  7: begin
       month  := 'July';
       season := 'Summer';
     end;
  10: begin
       month  := 'October';
       season := 'Fall';
     end;
  else
    begin
      month  := 'Not Beginning' +
          'of a quarter';
      season := 'undefined';
    end;
end;</pre> | <pre>switch (n) {
case 1:   month="January";
          season="winter";
          break;
case 4:   month="April";
          season="Spring";
          break;
case 7:   month="July";
          season="Summer";
          break;
case 10:  month="October";
          season="Fall";
          break;
default:  month="Not beginning"+
              "of a quarter";
          season="undefined";
}</pre> |

## 18. Decision Making with *switch*, *Select Case*, *Evaluate* or *case()of* Statements – Example 2

| FORTRAN | Visual Basic |
|---|---|
| ```
Select Case (M)
   Case (12,1,2)
     Season = 'winter'
   Case (3:5)
     Season = 'Spring'
   Case (6:8)
     Season = 'Summer'
   Case (9:11)
     Season = 'Fall'
   Case Default
     Season = 'Undefined'
End Select
``` | ```
Select Case M
   Case 12, 1, 2
       Season = "winter"
   Case 3, 4, 5
       Season = "Spring"
   Case 6, 7, 8
       Season = "Summer"
   Case 9, 10, 11
       Season = "Fall"
   Case Else
       Season = "Undefined"
End Select
``` |

**Decision Making with *switch*, *Select Case*, *Evaluate* or *case() of* Statements – Example 2**

| C | Java |
|---|---|
| ```
switch (n)
{
    case 12:
    case 1:
    case 2: strcpy(season, "winter");
            break;
    case 3:
    case 4:
    case 5: strcpy(season, "Spring");
            break;
    case 6:
    case 7:
    case 8: strcpy(season, "Summer");
            break;
    case 9:
    case 10:
    case 11: strcpy(season, "Fall");
            break;

    default: strcpy(season, "undefined");
}
``` | ```
switch (n) {
    case 12:
    case 1:
    case 2: season="winter";
            break;
    case 3:
    case 4:
    case 5: season="Spring";
            break;
    case 6:
    case 7:
    case 8: season="Summer";
            break;
    case 9:
    case 10:
    case 11: season="Fall";
            break;

    default: season="undefined";
}
``` |

## Decision Making with *switch*, *Select Case*, *Evaluate* or *case() of* Statements – Example 2

### COBOL

```
EVALUATE N
WHEN 12 ALSO 1 THRU 2
     MOVE "winter" TO SEASON
WHEN 3 THRU 5
     MOVE "Spring" TO SEASON
WHEN 6 THRU 8
     MOVE "Summer" TO SEASON
WHEN 9 THRU 11
     MOVE "Fall" TO SEASON
WHEN OTHER
       MOVE "undefined" TO SEASON
END-EVALUATE.
```

## Decision Making with *switch*, *Select Case*, *Evaluate* or *case() of* Statements – Example 2

### PASCAL

```
case n of
   12,
   1 ,
   2 : season := 'Winter';
   3 ,
   4 ,
   5 : season := 'Spring';
   6 ,
   7 ,
   8 : season := 'Summer';
   9 ,
   10,
   11: season := 'Fall';
 else
   season := 'Undefined' +
             ' Month';
end;
```

### Java

```
switch (n) {

    case 12:
    case 1:
    case 2: season="winter";
            break;
    case 3:
    case 4:
    case 5: season="Spring";
            break;
    case 6:
    case 7:
    case 8: season="Summer";
            break;
    case 9:
    case 10:
    case 11: season="Fall";
            break;

    default: season="undefined";
}
```

### 19. Looping Statements – Pre-test, Indeterminate – *while, perform until*

| FORTRAN | Visual Basic |
|---|---|
| ```
Do While (condition)
    statement1
    statement2
    :
    :
end Do
```<br><br>condition is a *boolean* expression.<br>It repeats the statement block as long as the *condition* is true. | ```
Do While condition
    statement1
    statement2
    :
    :
Loop
```<br><br>condition is a *boolean* expression.<br>It repeats the statement block as long as the *condition* is true. |
| ```
timeLeft = 5
Do While (timeLeft > 0)
    :
    timeLeft = timeLeft - 1
    :
End Do
``` | ```
timeLeft = 5
Do While timeLeft > 0
    ` other code
    timeLeft = timeLeft - 1
    ` other code
Loop
``` |

## Looping Statements – Pre-test, Indeterminate – *while, perform until*

| C | Java |
|---|---|
| `while (condition) statement1;`<br><br>or<br><br>`while (condition)`<br>`{`<br>`   statement1;`<br>`   statement2;`<br>`      :`<br>`      :`<br>`}`<br><br>*condition* can be any expression that evaluates to true (non-zero) or false (zero).<br>It repeats the statement or the statement block as long as the *condition* is true. | `while (condition) statement1;`<br><br>or<br><br>`while (condition){`<br>`   statement1;`<br>`   statement2;`<br>`      :`<br>`      :`<br>`}`<br><br>*condition* is a `boolean` expression.<br>It repeats the statement or the statement block as long as the *condition* is true. |
| `timeLeft=5;`<br>`while ( timeLeft > 0 )`<br>`{`<br>`   //other code`<br>`   timeLeft--;`<br>`   // other code`<br>`}` | `timeLeft=5;`<br>`while ( timeLeft > 0 ) {`<br>`   //other code`<br>`   timeLeft--;`<br>`   // other code`<br>`}` |

## Looping Statements – Pre-test, Indeterminate – `while, perform until`

### COBOL

```
PERFORM UNTIL CONDITION
    STATEMENT1
    STATEMENT2
      :
      :

END-PERFORM.
```

*condition* is a relational expression.
It repeats the statement block as long as the *condition* is true.

```
MOVE 5 TO TIME-LEFT
PEROFRM UNTIL TIME-LEFT> 0
      :
    SUBTRACT 1 FROM TIME-LEFT
      :
END-PERFORM.
```

## Looping Statements – Pre-test, Indeterminate – *while, perform until*

| PASCAL | Java |
|---|---|
| `while (condition) do statement1;`<br><br>or<br><br>`while (condition) do`<br>`begin`<br>`   statement1;`<br>`   statement2;`<br>`   :`<br>`   :`<br>`end;`<br><br>`condition` is a `boolean` expression.<br>It repeats the statement or the statement block as long as the `condition` is true. | `while (condition) statement1;`<br><br>or<br><br>`while (condition){`<br>`   statement1;`<br>`   statement2;`<br>`   :`<br>`   :`<br>`}`<br><br>`condition` is a `boolean` expression.<br>It repeats the statement or the statement block as long as the `condition` is true. |
| `timeLeft := 5;`<br>`while ( timeLeft > 0 ) do`<br>`begin`<br>`  // other code`<br>`  Dec(timeLeft);`<br>`  // other code`<br>`end;` | `timeLeft=5;`<br>`while ( timeLeft > 0 ) {`<br>`   //other code`<br>`   timeLeft--;`<br>`   // other code`<br>`}` |

## 20. Looping Statements – Post-test, Indeterminate – *do while, repeat*

| FORTRAN | Visual Basic |
|---|---|
| Fortran does not have a post-test indeterminate loop. | `Do`<br>    *statement1*<br>    *statement2*<br>    :<br>    :<br>`Loop While` *condition*<br><br>*condition* is a `boolean` expression.<br>It repeats the statement block as long as the *condition* is true.<br>Unlike the `Do While...Loop`, this loop executes at least once. |
|  | ```
timeLeft = 5
Do
    ' other code
    timeLeft = timeLeft - 1
    ' other code
Loop While timeLeft > 0
``` |
```

**Looping Statements – Post-test, Indeterminate –** `do while, repeat`

| C | Java |
|---|---|
| ```
do
    statement1;
while (condition);

or

do {

    statement1;
    statement2;
    :
    :
}while (condition);
```
**Notes:**
1. *condition* can be any expression that evaluates to true (non-zero) or false (zero)
2. it repeats the statement or the statement block as long as the *condition* is true
3. Unlike the `while` loop, the `do...while` loop is executed at least once. | ```
do
    statement1;
while (condition);

or

do {
    statement1;
    statement2;
    :
    :
}
while (condition);
```
**Notes:**
1. *condition* is a boolean expression
2. it repeats the statement or the statement block as long as the *condition* is true
3. Unlike the `while` loop, the `do...while` loop is executed at least once. |
| ```
timeLeft=5;
do
{
    //other code
    timeLeft--;
    // other code
}while ( timeLeft > 0 );
``` | ```
timeLeft=5;
do {
    //other code
    timeLeft--;
    // other code
}
while ( timeLeft > 0 );
``` |

**Looping Statements – Post-test, Indeterminate –** *do while, repeat*

## COBOL

Cobol does not have a post-test indeterminate loop.

| Looping Statements – Post-test, Indeterminate – *do while, repeat* | |
|---|---|
| **PASCAL** | **Java** |
| `repeat`<br>  `statement1;`<br>`until (condition);`<br><br>or<br><br>`repeat`<br>  `statement1;`<br>  `statement2;`<br>    `:`<br>    `:`<br>`until (condition);`<br><br>Notes:<br><br>1. `condition` is a `boolean` expression.<br>2. The last semicolon before `until` is optional.<br>3. It repeats the statement or the statement block as long as the `condition` is true. The `repeat` loop is executed at least once. | `do`<br>  `statement1;`<br>`while (condition);`<br><br>or<br><br>`do {`<br>  `statement1;`<br>  `statement2;`<br>    `:`<br>    `:`<br>`}`<br>`while (condition);`<br><br>Notes:<br><br>1. `condition` is a boolean expression.<br>2. It repeats the statement or the statement block as long as the `condition` is true.<br>3. Unlike the `while` loop, the `do...while` loop is executed at least once. |
| `timeLeft := 5;`<br>`repeat`<br>  `// Other Code`<br>  `Dec(timeLeft);`<br>  `// Other Code`<br>`until timeleft < 1 ;` | `timeLeft=5;`<br>`do {`<br>  `//other code`<br>  `timeLeft--;`<br>  `// other code`<br>`}`<br>`while ( timeLeft > 0 );` |

## 21. Looping Statements – Determinate – `do...enddo, for, for...next, perform times`

| FORTRAN | Visual Basic |
|---|---|
| `DO counter = start, stop [,step]`<br>    `statement1`<br>    `statement2`<br>    `:`<br>    `:`<br>`END DO`<br><br>**Remarks**<br><br>`counter` – a numeric variable<br>`start` – initial value of counter<br>`stop` – final value of counter<br>`step` – amount counter is changed at the end of every step (default step size is 1)<br><br>`counter, start, step` can be integers or floating point types | `For counter = start TO end [Step step]`<br>    `statement1`<br>    `statement2`<br>    `:`<br>    `:`<br>`Next [counter]`<br><br>**Remarks**<br><br>`counter` – a numeric variable<br>`start` – initial value of counter<br>`end` – final value of counter<br>`step` – amount counter is changed at the end of every step (default step size is 1)<br><br>`counter, start, step` can be integers or floating point types |
| The following loop prints numbers from 0 to 9<br><br>```
DO i = 0, 9, 1
    WRITE(*,*) I
END DO
``` | The following loop prints numbers from 0 to 9<br><br>```
For i = 0 To 9 Step 1
    Print i
Next I
``` |

## Looping Statements – Determinate – `do...enddo, for, for...next, perform times`

| C | Java |
|---|---|
| `for (initialization; condition; iteration)`<br>    `statement1;`<br><br>or<br><br>`for (initialization; condition; iteration)`<br>`{`<br>    `statement1;`<br>    `statement2;`<br>    `:`<br>`}`<br><br>Notes:<br><br>1. Initialization is executed first and only once.<br>2. `condition` (a relational expression) is evaluated, and if `true` the loop statements are executed.<br>3. Next, the `iteration` section is executed.<br>4. Steps 3 and 2 are repeated as long as the `condition` remains `true`. | `for (initialization; condition; iteration)`<br>    `statement1;`<br><br>or<br><br>`for (initialization; condition; iteration){`<br>    `statement1;`<br>    `statement2;`<br>    `:`<br>`}`<br><br>Notes:<br><br>1. `initialization` is executed first and only once.<br>2. `condition` (a boolean expression) is evaluated, and if `true` the loop statements are executed.<br>3. Next, the `iteration` section is executed.<br>4. Steps 3 and 2 are repeated as long as the `condition` remains `true`. |
| The following loop prints numbers from 0 to 9:<br><br>`for (int i=0; i<10; i++)`<br>`{`<br>    `printf(i,"\n");`<br>`}` | The following loop prints numbers from 0 to 9:<br><br>`for (int i=0; i<10; i++){`<br>    `System.out.println(i);`<br>`}` |

## Looping Statements – Determinate – *do...enddo, for, for...next, perform times*

### COBOL

```
PERFORM COUNT TIMES
   STATEMENT1
   STATEMENT2
   :
END-PRFORM.
```

COUNT - integer variable

The statements within the block are executed COUNT times.

---

The following loop prints numbers from 0 to 9:
```
MOVE 0 TO I
PERFORM 9 TIMES
   DISPLAY I
   ADD 1 TO I
END-PERFORM.
```

| Looping Statements – Determinate – `do...enddo`, `for`, `for...next`, `perform times` ||
|---|---|
| **PASCAL** | **Java** |
| `for counter := initialValue to finalValue do`<br>`statement`<br><br>or<br><br>`for counter := initialValue to finalValue do`<br>`begin`<br>  `statement1;`<br>  `statement2;`<br>    `:`<br>`end;`<br><br>1. `counter` is a local variable (declared in the block containing the for statement) of ordinal type, without any qualifiers.<br>2. `initialValue` and `finalValue` are expressions that are assignment-compatible with `counter`.<br>3. `statement` is a simple or structured statement that does not change the value of counter. | `for (initialization; condition; iteration)`<br>    `statement1;`<br><br>or<br><br>`for (initialization; condition; iteration){`<br>    `statement1;`<br>    `statement2;`<br>      `:`<br>`}`<br><br>**Notes:**<br><br>1. `initialization` is executed first and only once.<br>2. `condition` (a boolean expression) is evaluated, and if true the loop statements are executed.<br>3. Next, the `iteration` section is executed.<br>4. Steps 3 and 2 are repeated as long as the `condition` remains true. |
| The following loop prints numbers from 0 to 9:<br><br>`for i := 0 to 9 do`<br>`begin`<br>  `Writeln(i);`<br>`end;` | The following loop prints numbers from 0 to 9:<br><br>`for (int i=0; i<10; i++){`<br>    `System.out.println(i);`<br>`}` |

## 22. Looping Statements – Nested, Determinate – `do...enddo, for, for...next, perform times`

| FORTRAN | Visual Basic |
|---|---|
| In the following example, `j`-loop is nested within i-loop.<br><br>```
DO i = 1, 9
    DO j = 1, 9
        WRITE(*,*)   "X"
    END DO
    WRITE(*,*)
END DO
``` | In the following example, `j`-loop is nested within i-loop.<br><br>```
For i = 1 To 9
    For j = i To 9
        Print "*";
    Next j
    Print
Next I
``` |
| Multiple counters for a loop can be simulated as in the following example.<br><br>```
j = 100
DO i = 1, 9
    j = j - 2
    :
END DO
```<br><br>At the end of an iteration, `j` is decremented by two. | Multiple counters for a loop can be simulated as in the following example.<br><br>```
j = 100
For i = 1 To 9
    j = j - 2
Next I
```<br><br>At the end of an iteration, `j` is decremented by two. |

| Looping Statements – Nested, Determinate – *do...do, for, for...next, perform times* ||
|---|---|
| **C** | **Java** |
| In the following example, `j`-loop is nested within i-loop.<br><br>```c<br>for (int i=0; i<10; i++)<br>{<br>   for(int j=i; j<10; j++)<br>   {<br>      printf("*");<br>   }<br>   printf("\n");<br>}<br>``` | In the following example, `j`-loop is nested within i-loop.<br><br>```java<br>for (int i=0; i<10; i++) {<br>   for(int j=i; j<10; j++) {<br>      System.out.print("*");<br>   }<br>   System.out.println();<br>}<br>``` |
| `for` loops can also have multiple initializers:<br><br>```c<br>for (int i=1, j=100; i<10; i++, j=j-2){<br>   :<br>   :<br>}<br>```<br><br>In the above loop, at the end of each iteration, `i` is incremented by one and `j` is decremented by two. | `for` loops can also have multiple initializers:<br><br>```java<br>for (int i=1, j=100; i<10; i++, j=j-2){<br>   :<br>   :<br>}<br>```<br><br>In the above loop, at the end of each iteration, `i` is incremented by one and `j` is decremented by two. |

## Looping Statements – Nested, Determinate – *do...enddo, for, for...next, perform times*

### COBOL

In the following example, `j`-loop is nested within `i`-loop.

```
PERFORM DISPLAY-Para VARYING I FROM 1 BY 1
        UNTIL I > 9
        AFTER J VARYING FROM 1 BY 1
           UNTIL J > 4
DISPLAY-Para.
   Statement1
   Statement2.
```

Multiple counters for a loop can be simulated as in the following example.

```
MOVE 100 TO J.
MOVE 1 TO I.
PERFORM UNTIL I > 10
     COMPUTE J = J - 2
     COMPUTE I = 1 + 1
     DISPLAY "I = " , I
     DISPLAY "J= ", J
END-PERFORM.
```

At the end of an iteration, `I` is incremented by one and `J` is decremented by two.

**Looping Statements – Nested, Determinate –** *do...enddo, for, for...next, perform times*

| PASCAL | Java |
|---|---|
| In the following example, `j`-loop is nested within `i`-loop.<br><br>```<br>for i := 0 to 9 do<br>begin<br>  for j = i to 9 do<br>  begin<br>    Write('*');<br>  end;<br>  Writeln('');<br>end;<br>``` | In the following example, `j`-loop is nested within `i`-loop.<br><br>```<br>for (int i=0; i<10; i++) {<br>    for(int j=i; j<10; j++) {<br>        System.out.print("*");<br>    }<br>    System.out.println();<br>}<br>``` |
| Multiple counters for a loop can be simulated as in the following example.<br><br>```<br>j := 100;<br>for i := 0 to 9 do<br>begin<br>   j := j-2;<br>   ` other statements<br>end;<br>```<br><br>In the above loop, at the end of each iteration, `i` is incremented by one and `j` is decremented by two. | The `for` loops can also have multiple initializers:<br><br>```<br>for (int i=1, j=100; i<10; i++, j=j-2){<br>    :<br>    :<br>}<br>```<br><br>In the above loop, at the end of each iteration, `i` is incremented by one and `j` is decremented by two. |

## 23. Nested Loops – Ways of Terminating

| FORTRAN | Visual Basic |
|---|---|
| ``` Program NestDo DO I=1,5    DO J=I,3    WRITE(*,*) 'I=',I,',J=',J    IF((I+J).GT.4) GO TO 10    END DO END DO 10      CONTINUE stop end ``` | ``` Private Sub Command1_Click() For I = 1 To 5    For J = I To 3       Print "i=" & I & "j=" & J       If (I + J) > 4 Then GoTo xyz    Next J Next I xyz: : : End Sub ``` |
| In the above example, `j`-loop is nested within `i`-loop. A `GoTo` statement is used to break out the nested loops.<br><br>The output of the above example will be as follows:<br><br>i=1,j=1<br>i=1,j=2<br>i=1,j=3<br>i=2,j=2<br>i=2,j=3 | In the above example, `j`-loop is nested within `i`-loop. A label `xyz` is defined at the end of the loop. A `GoTo` statement is used to break out the nested loops.<br><br>The output of the above example will be as follows:<br><br>i=1,j=1<br>i=1,j=2<br>i=1,j=3<br>i=2,j=2<br>i=2,j=3 |

## Nested Loops – Ways of Terminating

| C | Java |
|---|---|
| ```
#include <stdio.h>
int main()
{
    int i, j;
    for (i = 1; i <= 5; i++)
    {
        for (j = i; j <= 3; j++)
        {
            printf("i=%d,j=%d\n",i,j);
            if ((i+j) > 4) goto xyz;
        }
    }
    xyz:
    return 0;
}
``` | ```
class NestedLoops2 {
  public static void main(String args[]) {

    xyz: for (int i=1; i<=5; i++) {
      for(int j=i; j<=3; j++) {
        System.out.println("i="+i+",j="+j);
        if ((i+j)>4){
          break xyz;
        } // end of if block
      } // end of inner loop
    } // end of outer loop
  } // end of main
}
``` |
| In the above example, `j`-loop is nested within `i`-loop. A label done is defined at the end of the loop. A `goto` statement is used to break out the nested loops.<br><br>The output of the above example will be as follows:<br><br>i=1,j=1<br>i=1,j=2<br>i=1,j=3<br>i=2,j=2<br>i=2,j=3 | In the above example, `j`-loop is nested within `i`-loop. The outer `i`-loop is labeled as `xyz`. Within the inner loop, break `xyz` statement terminates the outer loop.<br><br>The output of the above example will be as follows:<br><br>i=1,j=1<br>i=1,j=2<br>i=1,j=3<br>i=2,j=2<br>i=2,j=3 |

### Nested Loops – Ways of Terminating

**COBOL**

```
PERFORM DISP-COUNT THRU DISP-COUNT-EXIT
        VARYING I FROM 1 BY 1
        UNTIL I > 5
        AFTER VARYING J FROM 1 BY 1
        UNTIL J > 3
        DISP-COUNT.
           DISPLAY "I=" I "J=" J
             IF J=3 GO TO DISP-COUNT-EXIT.
           DISP-COUNT-EXIT.   EXIT.
```

In the above example, j-loop is nested within i-loop. A GoTo statement is used to break out the nested loops.

The output of the above example will be as follows:

```
i=1,j=1
i=1,j=2
i=1,j=3
i=2,j=2
i=2,j=3
```

## Nested Loops – Ways of Terminating

| PASCAL | Java |
|---|---|
| ```
program breaknested;
{$APPTYPE CONSOLE}
uses
  SysUtils;
var
  i, j : Integer;
  label xyz;
begin
  for i := 1 to 5 do
    for j := i to 3 do
    begin
      Writeln('i=' + IntToStr(i) + ', j=' +
                    IntToStr(j));
      if (i + J) > 4 then
        goto xyz;
    end;
  one:
end.
``` | ```
class NestedLoops2 {
  public static void main(String args[]) {

    xyz: for (int i=1; i<=5; i++) {
      for(int j=i; j<=3; j++) {
        System.out.println("i="+i+",j="+j);
        if ((i+j)>4){
          break xyz;
        } // end of if block
      } // end of inner loop
    } // end of outer loop
  } // end of main
}
``` |
| In the above example, j-loop is nested within i-loop. The outer i-loop is labeled as xyz. Within the inner loop, goto statement terminates the outer loop.<br><br>The output of the above example will be as follows:<br><br>i=1,   j=1<br>i=1,   j=2<br>i=1,   j=3<br>i=2,   j=2<br>i=2,   j=3 | In the above example, j-loop is nested within i-loop. The outer i-loop is labeled as xyz. Within the inner loop, break xyz statement terminates the outer loop.<br><br>The output of the above example will be as follows:<br><br>i=1,j=1<br>i=1,j=2<br>i=1,j=3<br>i=2,j=2<br>i=2,j=3 |

## 24. Other Ways of Making a Selection

| FORTRAN | Visual Basic |
|---|---|
| Use the block form of `If`. | `If condition Then statement1 Else Statement2`<br><br>`condition1` is a `boolean` expression<br><br>If `condition1` is true, `statement1` is evaluated. Otherwise, `statement2` is evaluated. |
| | `If (a < b) Then fraction = a / b Else fraction = b / a`<br><br>In the above example, if the `boolean` expression (`a < b`) is true then fraction is calculated as `a/b`, otherwise fraction is calculated as `b/a`<br><br>The above statements can also be written as follows:<br><br>`If (a < b) Then`<br>`    fraction = a/b`<br>`Else`<br>`    fraction = b/a`<br>`End If` |

## Other Ways of Making a Selection

| C | Java |
|---|---|
| ? operator<br><br>*expression1* & *expression2* : *expression3*<br><br>Where<br><br>*expression1* – any relational expression<br>*expression2*, *expression3* – any expressions that return the same type | ? operator<br><br>*expression1* & *expression2* : *expression3*<br><br>Where<br><br>*expression1* – any boolean expression<br>*expression2*, *expression3* – any expressions that return the same type |
| `fraction = (a <b ) ? (a/b) : (b/a)`<br><br>In the above example, if the `relational` expression (a < b) is true then the expression between ? and : is evaluated. If (a < b) is false then the expression to the right of : is evaluated.<br><br>The above statement can also be written using if as follows:<br><br>```
if (a < b)
{
   fraction = a/b;
}
else
{
   fraction = b/a;
}
``` | `fraction = (a <b ) ? (a/b) : (b/a)`<br><br>In the above example, if the `relational` expression (a < b) is true then the expression between ? and : is evaluated. If (a < b) is false then the expression to the right of : is evaluated.<br><br>The above statement can also be written using if as follows:<br><br>```
if (a < b) {
   fraction = a/b;
}
else {
   fraction = b/a;
}
``` |

**Other Ways of Making a Selection**

### COBOL

Use `IF...ELSE` statement

## Other Ways of Making a Selection

| PASCAL | Java |
|---|---|
| Use `if` statement. | `?` operator<br><br>*expression1* & *expression2* : *expression3*<br><br>Where<br><br>*expression1* – any boolean expression<br>*expression2, expression3* – any expression that return the same type |
| | `fraction = (a <b ) ? (a/b) : (b/a)`<br><br>In the above example, if the `relational` expression `(a < b)` is true then the expression between ? and : is evaluated. If `(a < b)` is false then the expression to the right of : is evaluated.<br><br>The above statement can also be written using if as follows:<br><br>```
if (a < b) {
    fraction = a/b;
}
else {
    fraction = b/a;
}
``` |
```

## 25. Read/Write from the Console

| FORTRAN | Visual Basic |
|---|---|
| ```
Program ReadConsole
Double Precision x,y
write(*,*)
& 'Enter a number'
Read(*,*) x
y = 1.5 * x
write(*,*) 'x=',' 1.5x=',y
stop
end
``` | ```
Private Sub Command1_Click()
Dim x As Double, y As Double
Dim linex As String
x = 1
Do While (x > 0)
    linex = InputBox("Enter a number", _
                            "Input", "1.0")
    x = CDbl(linex)
    y = 1.5 * x
    Print "x = " & x & "  1.5x = ", y
Loop
End Sub
``` |

## Read/Write from the Console

| C | Java |
|---|---|
| ```c
#include <stdio.h>

#include <stdlib.h>
/* This program prompts the user to enter
   a number of the type double, then prints
   the entered number and also its value
   multiplied by 1.5
*/
int main()
{
    double x = 1.0, y;
    char line[80];
    while (x > 0)
    {
        printf(
        "Enter a floating point number\n");
        scanf("%s", line);
        x = strtod(line, (char **)NULL);
        y = 1.5 * x;
        printf("x = %f   1.5x = %f\n",
                x, y);
    }
    return 0;
}
``` | ```java
import java.io.*;
/* This program prompts the user to enter
   a number of the type double, then prints
   the entered number and also its value
   multiplied by 1.5
*/
class ReadDouble {
  public static void main(String
args[])throws IOException
    {
    BufferedReader inData = new
            BufferedReader(new
            InputStreamReader(System.in));
    double x=1.0,y;
    String line;
    while(x > 0) {
    System.out.println(
        "Enter a floating point number.");

        line = inData.readLine();
        x = Double.parseDouble(line);
        y = 1.5 * x;

        System.out.println("x = " + x +
                "    1.5x = " + y);
    }
  }
}
``` |

99

## Read/Write from the Console

### COBOL

```
        IDENTIFICATION DIVISION.
*------------------------------------
        PROGRAM-ID.             DOUBLEP.
*------------------------------------
*   This program prompts user to enter
*   a number of type double,
*   then prints the entered number and
*  also its value multiplied by 1.5
$PAGE "WORKING STORAGE Section"
        DATA DIVISION.
*------------------------------------
        WORKING-STORAGE SECTION.
*------------------------------------

        01 ACCEPT-STRING.
           05 ACCEPT-NUMBER               PIC 9(06).
           05 ACCEPT-NUMBER-N REDEFINES   ACCEPT-NUMBER
                                          PIC 9(04)V9(02).
           05 FILLER                      PIC X(74).

        01 DISPLAY-STRING .
           05 DISPLAY-NUMBER              PIC Z(5)9.99 .

        01 COMPUTED-NUMBER                PIC 9(04)V9(02) COMP.
*------------------------------------
        PROCEDURE DIVISION.
*------------------------------------

        0000-MAIN.
       *---------
           DISPLAY SPACES.
           DISPLAY "Enter a double number or 9999 to terminate".
           ACCEPT ACCEPT-NUMBER.
           IF ACCEPT-NUMBER EQUAL 9999
              STOP RUN.
           MOVE ACCEPT-NUMBER-N TO COMPUTED-NUMBER
           COMPUTE DISPLAY-NUMBER ROUNDED =
                              COMPUTED-NUMBER  * 1.5

           DISPLAY "You have entered = " ACCEPT-NUMBER
              "  1.5 Times of this number is = " DISPLAY-NUMBER.
        0000-EXIT. EXIT.
```

## Read/Write from the Console

| PASCAL | Java |
|---|---|
| ```
program ReadDouble;
{$APPTYPE CONSOLE}
{ This program prompts the user to enter
  a number of the type double, then prints
  the entered number and also its value
  multiplied by 1.5
}
uses
  SysUtils;
var
  line : string;
  x, y : double;
begin
  writeln('Enter a floating point number.');
  Read  (line);
  writeln('');
  x := StrToFloat(line);
  y := 1.5 * x;
  write('x = ' + FloatToStr(x) + '    1.5x = ' + FloatToStr(y));
end.
``` | ```
import java.io.*;
/* This program prompts the user to enter
   a number of the type double, then prints
   the entered number and also its value
   multiplied by 1.5
*/
class ReadDouble {
  public static void main(String args[])throws IOException
    {
      BufferedReader inData = new
            BufferedReader(new
            InputStreamReader(System.in));
      double x=1.0,y;
      String line;
      while(x > 0) {
      System.out.println(
           "Enter a floating point number.");

           line = inData.readLine();
           x = Double.parseDouble(line);
           y = 1.5 * x;

           System.out.println("x = " + x +
                "    1.5x = " + y);
      }
    }
}
``` |

## 26. Write to a Sequential File

| FORTRAN | Visual Basic |
|---|---|
| These programs write six pairs of numbers, each pair consisting of an integer and a double to file `f.dat`. The file is of the binary type. The next example reads the data from the file `f.dat`. | These programs write six pairs of numbers, each pair consisting of an integer and a double to file `f.dat`. The file is of the binary type. The next example reads the data from the file `f.dat`. |

<table>
<tr>
<td>

```
      DOUBLE PRECISION DATS(6)
      INTEGER IDATS(6)
      DATA DATS
     & /3.1, 2.1, 4.5, 7.9, 11.0, 7.5/
      DATA IDATS/33, 45, 88, 1, 5, 7/
      OPEN(7, FILE='F.DAT',FORM='BINARY')
      DO I=1,6
         WRITE(7) DATS(I),IDATS(I)
      END DO
      CLOSE(7)
      STOP
      END
```

</td>
<td>

```
Private Sub Command1_Click()
Dim dats(5) As Double
Dim idats(5) As Integer
Dim I As Integer
dats(0) = 3.1: dats(1) = 2.1: dats(2) = 4.5
dats(3) = 7.9: dats(4) = 11#: dats(5) = 7.5
idats(0) = 33: idats(1) = 45: idats(2) = 88
idats(3) = 1: idats(4) = 5: idats(5) = 7
Open "f.dat" For Output As 1
For I = 0 To 5
    Print #1, dats(I)
    Print #1, idats(I)
Next I
Close #1
End Sub
```

</td>
</tr>
</table>

## Write to a Sequential File

### C

```c
#include <stdio.h>
/* This program writes six pairs of numbers,
each pair consisting of an integer and a
double to the file f.dat.
The file is of the binary type. The next
example reads the data from the file f.dat
*/
int main()
{
    double dats[] =
        {3.1,2.1,4.5,7.9,11.0,7.5};
    int idats[] = {33,45,88,1,5,7};
    int i;
    FILE* fo;
    fo = fopen("f.dat", "w");
    for (i = 0; i < 6; i ++)
    {
      fwrite(&dats[i], sizeof(double),1,fo);
      fwrite(&idats[i], sizeof(int), 1, fo);
    }
    fclose(fo);
    return 0;
}
```

### Java

```java
/* This program writes six pairs of numbers,
each pair consisting of an integer and a
double to the file f.dat.
The file is of the binary type. The next
example reads the data from the file f.dat
*/
import java.io.*;

class FileOut {
   public static void main(String args[])
              throws Exception {
      double dats[] =
          {3.1,2.1,4.5,7.9,11.0,7.5};
      int idats[] = {33,45,88,1,5,7};
      FileOutputStream fo =
          new FileOutputStream("f.dat");
      DataOutputStream outData =
             new DataOutputStream(fo);
      for (int i=0; i <6; i++) {
         outData.writeDouble(dats[i]);
         outData.writeInt(idats[i]);
      }
      fo.close();
   }
}
```

## Write to a Sequential File

### COBOL

```cobol
       IDENTIFICATION DIVISION.
      *------------------------
       PROGRAM-ID. FILEOUTP.
      *------------------------
      * This program writes six pairs of numbers
      * in a file called f.dat. The int & the
      * double numbers are written alternately.
      * The file is of text type with sequential
      * file organization
      * The next example will read data from f.dat.
      *-----------------
       ENVIRONMENT DIVISION.
       CONFIGURATION SECTION.
       SOURCE-COMPUTER.
       OBJECT-COMPUTER.
       INPUT-OUTPUT SECTION.
       FILE-CONTROL.

       SELECT OUTFILE             ASSIGN TO FDAT
       FILE STATUS IS WS-STAT.
      *------------------------
       DATA DIVISION.
      *------------------------
       FILE SECTION.

       FD OUTFILE .
       01 OUTFILE-REC                  PIC X(80).
       $PAGE "WORKING STORAGE Section"
      *------------------------
       WORKING-STORAGE SECTION.
      *------------------------
       01 WS-STAT       PIC XX VALUE SPACES.
       01 WS-REC.
           05 WS-ARRAY OCCURS 6 TIMES.
              10 WS-DBL-NO     PIC 99V9.
              10 WS-INT-NO     PIC 99.
       01 FILLER-1           PIC X(18) VALUE
           "031021045079110075".
        01 DBL-ARRAY REDEFINES   FILLER-1.
           05 DBL-ARRAY-A PIC 99V9 OCCURS 6 TIMES.
        01 FILLER-2           PIC X(12) VALUE
           "334588010507".
        01 INT-ARRAY REDEFINES FILLER-2.
           05 INT-ARRAY-A  PIC 99 OCCURS 6 TIMES.
        01 W-CNT             PIC 99 COMP VALUE 0.
       *------------------------
       PROCEDURE DIVISION
       *------------------------
       0000-MAIN.
           DISPLAY SPACES.
           OPEN OUTPUT OUTFILE.
           IF WS-STAT <> "00"
              DISPLAY "ERROR OPENING FDAT FILE"
              STOP RUN.
           PERFORM WRITE-FILE THRU WRITE-FILE-EXIT
           STOP RUN.
       0000-EXIT. EXIT.
       WRITE-FILE.
             MOVE SPACES TO OUTFILE-REC
             PERFORM FILL-ARRAY THRU FILL-ARRAY-EXIT
                    VARYING W-CNT FROM 1 BY 1 UNTIL
                       W-CNT > 6.
             MOVE WS-REC TO OUTFILE-REC
             WRITE OUTFILE-REC.
       WRITE-FILE-EXIT. EXIT.
       FILL-ARRAY.
          MOVE DBL-ARRAY-A(W-CNT) TO WS-DBL-NO(W-CNT)
          MOVE INT-ARRAY-A(W-CNT) TO WS-INT-NO(W-CNT).
       FILL-ARRAY-EXIT. EXIT.
```

## Write to a Sequential File

| PASCAL | Java |
|---|---|
| ```pascal
program FileOut;
{$APPTYPE CONSOLE}
{ This program writes six pairs numbers to
  the file f.dat. The int and double numbers
  are written alternately. The file is of
  the binary type. The next example reads
  the data from the file f.dat.
}
uses
 SysUtils;
var
 ddats : array [0..5] of double =
(3.1,2.1,4.5,7.9,11.0,7.5);
 idats : array [0..5] of integer = (33, 45,
88, 1, 5, 7);
 fo    : FILE;
 i     : Integer;
begin
 AssignFile(fo,'f.dat');
 Rewrite(fo, 8);     { Record size = 1 }
 for i  := 0 to 5 do
 begin
   BlockWrite(fo,ddats[i],1);
   BlockWrite(fo,idats[i],1);
 end;
 CloseFile(fo);
end.
``` | ```java
/* This program writes six pairs of numbers,
each pair consisting of an integer and a
double to the file f.dat.
The file is of the binary type. The next
example reads the data from the file f.dat
*/
import java.io.*;

class FileOut {
   public static void main(String args[])
            throws Exception {
      double dats[] =
         {3.1,2.1,4.5,7.9,11.0,7.5};
      int idats[] = {33,45,88,1,5,7};
      FileOutputStream fo =
         new FileOutputStream("f.dat");
      DataOutputStream outData =
         new DataOutputStream(fo);
      for (int i=0; i <6; i++) {
      outData.writeDouble(dats[i]);
      outData.writeInt(idats[i]);
      }
      fo.close();
   }
}
``` |

## 27. Read from a Sequential File

| FORTRAN | Visual Basic |
|---|---|
| ```
DOUBLE PRECISION DATS
INTEGER IDATS
OPEN(7, FILE='F.DAT',FORM='BINARY')
DO I=1,6
   READ(7) DATS,IDATS
   WRITE(*,*) DATS, IDATS
END DO
CLOSE(7)
STOP
END
``` | ```
Private Sub Command2_Click()
Dim ddat As Double
Dim idat As Integer
Dim I As Integer
Open "f.dat" For Input As 1
For I = 0 To 5
   Input #1, ddat
   Input #1, idat
Print ddat, idat
Next I
Close #1
End Sub
``` |

## Read a Sequential File

| C | Java |
|---|---|
| ```c
#include <stdio.h>
/* This program reads the file created
   in the previous example, and prints
   the data read from the file
*/
int main()
{
    int idat, i;
    double ddat;
    FILE *fi;
    fi = fopen("f.dat", "r");
    for (i = 0; i < 6; i ++)
    {
        fread(&ddat, sizeof(double), 1, fi);
        fread(&idat, sizeof(int), 1, fi);
        printf("%lf   %d\n", ddat, idat);
    }
    fclose(fi);
    return 0;
}
``` | ```java
/* This program reads the file created in
   the previous example, and prints
   the data read from the file
*/
import java.io.*;

class FileIn {
  public static void main (String args[])
      throws Exception{
    int idat;
    double ddat;
    FileInputStream fi=
        new FileInputStream("f.dat");
    DataInputStream inData =
        new DataInputStream(fi);
    for (int i=0; i <6; i++) {
       ddat = inData.readDouble();
       idat = inData.readInt();
       System.out.println(ddat + "    " +
                                    idat);
    }
    fi.close();
  }
}
``` |

## Read a Sequential File

### COBOL

```cobol
        IDENTIFICATION DIVISION.
*--------------------------
        PROGRAM-ID. FILEINP.
*--------------------------
*--------------------------
*   This program reads the file created
*   in the previous example, & prints
*   the data read from the file f.dat
*   The file is of text type with sequential
*   file organization
*----------------------------------------------
        ENVIRONMENT DIVISION.
        CONFIGURATION SECTION.
        INPUT-OUTPUT SECTION.
        FILE-CONTROL.
        SELECT OUTFILE              ASSIGN TO FDAT
        FILE STATUS IS WS-STAT.
*--------------------------
        DATA DIVISION.
*--------------------------
        FILE SECTION.

        FD OUTFILE .
        01 OUTFILE-REC                  PIC X(80).
$PAGE "WORKING STORAGE Section"
*--------------------------
        WORKING-STORAGE SECTION.
*--------------------------
        01 WS-STAT              PIC XX VALUE SPACES.
        01 WS-REC.
           05 WS-ARRAY OCCURS   6 TIMES.
              10 WS-DBL-NO      PIC 99V9.
              10 WS-INT-NO      PIC 99.
        01 DISPLAY-LINE.
           05 PRINT-ARRAY  OCCURS 6 TIMES.
              10 P-DBL-NO       PIC Z9.9B.
              10 P-INT-NO       PIC Z9B.
        01 W-CNT                PIC 99 COMP VALUE 0.
        01 EOF                  PIC X VALUE SPACES.
*--------------------------
        PROCEDURE DIVISION
        0000-MAIN.
            DISPLAY SPACES.
            OPEN INPUT   OUTFILE.
            IF WS-STAT <> "00"
               DISPLAY "ERROR OPENING FDAT FILE"
               STOP RUN.
            PERFORM PRINT-FILE THRU PRINT-FILE-EXIT
            CLOSE OUTFILE
            STOP RUN.
        0000-EXIT. EXIT.
        PRINT-FILE.
            MOVE SPACES TO WS-REC DISPLAY-LINE
            READ OUTFILE
                AT END
                    MOVE "Y" TO EOF.
            IF EOF <> "Y"
               MOVE OUTFILE-REC TO WS-REC
               PERFORM FILL-ARRAY THRU FILL-ARRAY-EXIT
                   VARYING W-CNT FROM 1 BY 1 UNTIL
                       W-CNT > 6.
            DISPLAY SPACES
            DISPLAY DISPLAY-LINE

        PRINT-FILE-EXIT. EXIT.
        FILL-ARRAY.
            MOVE WS-DBL-NO(W-CNT)   TO P-DBL-NO (W-CNT)
            MOVE WS-INT-NO(W-CNT)   TO P-INT-NO (W-CNT).
        FILL-ARRAY-EXIT. EXIT.
```

## Read a Sequential File

| PASCAL | Java |
|---|---|
| ```pascal
program FileIn;
{$APPTYPE CONSOLE}
{ This program reads the file created
  in the previous example, and prints
  the data read from the file.
}
uses
 SysUtils;
var
 idat : Integer;
 ddat : Double;
 fi   : FILE;
 i    : Integer;
begin
 AssignFile(fi,'f.dat');
 Reset(fi,8);
 for i   := 0 to 5 do
 begin
   BlockRead(fi,ddat,1);
   BlockRead(fi,idat,1);
   Writeln(FloatToStr(ddat) + ' ' +
IntToStr(idat));
 end;
 CloseFile(fi);
end.
``` | ```java
/* This program reads the file created
   in the previous example, and prints
   the data read from the file
*/

import java.io.*;

class FileIn {
  public static void main (String args[])
     throws Exception{
     int idat;
     double ddat;
     FileInputStream fi=
          new FileInputStream("f.dat");
     DataInputStream inData =
          new DataInputStream(fi);
     for (int i=0; i <6; i++) {
        ddat = inData.readDouble();
        idat = inData.readInt();
        System.out.println(ddat + "   " +
                                       idat);
     }
     fi.close();
  }
}
``` |

109

## 28. Read/Write from a Binary Random File

| FORTRAN | Visual Basic |
|---|---|
| ```
      PROGRAM FILERAND
      REAL*4 X(6), Z
      INTEGER I
      DATA X/3.5, 4.9, 99.0, 3.9,
     &      7.6, 2.3/
      OPEN(9, FILE='X.DAT', RECL=4,
     &   FORM='UNFORMATTED',
     &   ACCESS='DIRECT')
      DO I = 1, 6
         WRITE(9 ,REC=I) X(I)
      ENDDO
C     READ THE THIRD  RECORD
      READ(9,REC=3) Z
      WRITE(*,*) Z
C     READ THE FIFTH RECORD
      READ(9,REC=5) Z
      WRITE(*,*) Z
      CLOSE(9)
      STOP
      END
``` | ```
Private Sub Command3_Click()
Dim x(5) As Double
Dim I As Integer
Dim y As Double
x(0) = 3.5: x(1) = 4.9: x(2) = 99#
x(3) = 3.9: x(4) = 7.6: x(5) = 2.3
Open "x.dat" For Random As 1 Len = 8
For I = 0 To 5
    Put #1, I + 1, x(I)
Next I
' now read 3rd number from the file
Get #1, 3, y
Print y
' now read 5th number from the file
Get #1, 5, y
Print y
Close #1
End Sub
``` |
| The output of the program:<br><br>99.0<br>7.6 | The output of the program:<br><br>99.0<br>7.6 |

### Read/Write from a Binary Random File

| C | Java |
|---|---|
| ```c
#include <stdio.h>
int main()
{
    float x[] = {3.5f, 4.9f, 99.0f, 3.9f, 7.6f, 2.3f};
    FILE *f;
    float val;
    f = fopen("x.dat", "w+");
    fwrite(x, sizeof(float), 6, f);
    rewind(f);
    fseek(f, sizeof(float) * 2, SEEK_SET);
    fread(&val, sizeof(float), 1, f);
    printf("%f\n", val);
    rewind(f);
    fseek(f, sizeof(float) * 4, SEEK_SET);
    fread(&val, sizeof(float), 1, f);
    printf("%f\n", val);
    fclose(f);
    return 0;
}
``` | ```java
/* This program writes several numbers to a
   file (x.dat). the file pointer is
   repositioned and the third and the fifth
   numbers are read and printed.
*/
import java.io.*;
class FileRand {
    public static void main(String args[])
            throws Exception {
        float x[]=
        {3.5f, 4.9f, 99.0f, 3.9f, 7.6f, 2.3f};

        RandomAccessFile f=new
                RandomAccessFile("x.dat","rw");

        for (int i=0; i<x.length;i++){
            f.writeFloat(x[i]);
        }
        f.seek(8); // Skip 8 bytes from
                   // the beginning
        System.out.println(f.readFloat());

        f.seek(16);// Skip 16 bytes from
                   // the beginning
        System.out.println(f.readFloat());
    }
}
``` |

### Read/Write from a Binary Random File

**COBOL**

Binary files are not commonly used in Cobol.

## Read/Write from a Binary Random File

| PASCAL | Java |
|---|---|
| ```pascal
program FileRand;
{$APPTYPE CONSOLE}
uses
   SysUtils;
{ This program writes several numbers to a
  file (x.dat). The file is then rewound
  and the third and fifth numbers
  are read.
}
var
  x : array [0..5] of single = (3.5, 4.9,
                    99.0, 3.9, 7.6, 2.3);
  y : single;
  f : FILE;
  i : Integer;
begin
  AssignFile(f,'x.dat');
  rewrite(f, 4);
  for i := 0 to 5 do
  begin
    blockwrite(f,x[i],1);
  end;
  reset(f, 4);
  seek(f,2);
  blockread(f,y,1);
  Writeln(FloatToStr(y));
  seek(f,4);
  blockread(f,y,1);
  Writeln(FloatToStr(y));
end.
``` | ```java
/* This program writes several numbers to a
   file (x.dat). the file pointer is
   repositioned and the third and the fifth
   numbers are read and printed.
*/
import java.io.*;
class FileRand {
   public static void main(String args[])
           throws Exception {
     float x[]=
     {3.5f, 4.9f, 99.0f, 3.9f, 7.6f, 2.3f};

     RandomAccessFile f=new
          RandomAccessFile("x.dat","rw");

     for (int i=0; i<x.length;i++){
        f.writeFloat(x[i]);
     }
     f.seek(8); // Skip 8 bytes from
                // the beginning
     System.out.println(f.readFloat());

     f.seek(16);// Skip 16 bytes from
                // the beginning
     System.out.println(f.readFloat());
   }
}
``` |

## 29. Define and use a Method (Function)

| FORTRAN | Visual Basic |
|---|---|
| Syntax:<br><br>`Function functionName([paramlist])`<br>`  statements`<br>`  functionName` = returnValue<br>`  return`<br>`End`<br><br>`returnType` – return type of the function. It is always required.<br>`functionName` – is the name of the function.<br><br>The value to be returned from a function is assigned to the `functionName`.<br>A `return` statement is used to return from the function.<br>`End` is the end of the function.<br><br>The function ends when it encounters `End` statement. `Exit` statement can be used to return out of a function sooner.<br><br>Note: A Subroutine can also be defined in Fortran. A Subroutine does not return a value, it can, however, return parameters if passed by reference. | Syntax:<br><br>`Function functionName([paramlist]) as returnType`<br>`  statements`<br>`  functionName = returnValue`<br>`End Function`<br><br>`returnType` – return type of the function. It is always required.<br>`functionName` – is the name of the function.<br><br>The value to be returned from a function is assigned to the `functionName`.<br><br>The function ends when it encounters `End Function` statement. `Exit Function` statement can be used to return out of a function sooner.<br><br>Note: A `Sub` procedure can also be defined in Visual Basic. A `Sub` does not return a value, it can, however, return parameters if passed by reference. |

## Define and use a Method (Function)

| C | Java |
|---|---|
| Syntax:<br><br>`returnType functionName([parameterList]) {`<br>`    statements`<br>`}`<br><br>`returnType` – return type of a function. If a function does not return anything, use void.<br>`functionName` – is the name of the function.<br><br>Functions can accept parameters. Each parameter is specified by its type and a variable. The variable becomes the local variable for the function.<br><br>A `return` statement is used to return from the function or return a value from the function.<br><br>A `return` statement is optional in a function with return type void.<br><br>A `return` statement is required for a function with a return type other than void. | Java does not have global functions. Functions are always part of a java class. In Java, functions are called either member functions or methods.<br><br>Syntax:<br><br>`returnType functionName([parameterList]) {`<br>`    statements`<br>`}`<br><br>`returnType` – return type of a method. It is always required. If a method does not return anything, use void.<br>`functionName` – is the name of the method.<br><br>Methods can accept parameters. Each parameter is specified by its type and a variable. The variable becomes the local variable for the method.<br><br>A `return` statement is used to return from the method or return a value from the method.<br><br>A `return` statement is optional in a method with return type void.<br><br>A `return` statement is required for a method with a return type other than void. |

### Define and use a Method (Function)

## COBOL

The concept of calling a function is implemented by Cobol in the form of a subprogram. There is only one main program and one or more subprograms. The variables defined in the subprogram are local variables for that subprogram.

The subprogram is called by the main program using the `CALL` statement. The main difference between a main program and subprogram is that unlike the main program which should have a `STOP RUN` statement somewhere, in the subprogram a special verb `EXIT PROGRAM` or `GOBACK` is used.

Exanple:

```
Main Program.
.
.
.
Call 'SUB-A'.
.
.
Call 'SUB-B'.
STOP RUN.
Subprogram SUB-A.
.
.
.
EXIT PROGRAM.
.
```

In the above example the main program calls subprogram `SUB-A`

The main program always calls a subprogram by passing parameters by reference. The common data or link data between the main program and the subprogram has to be specified in both these program. Further a special `LINKAGE SECTION` in `DATA DIVISION` of a subprogram is used to define the data involved in both program.

## Define and use a Method (Function)

| PASCAL | Java |
|---|---|
| Syntax:<br><br>`function functionName([paramList]): rType`<br>`begin`<br>`    statements`<br>`end;`<br><br>where<br><br>`function` -- keyword signaling the beginning of the function.<br>`functionName` -- name of the function.<br>`rType` -- return data type of the function.<br>The value to be returned from a function is assigned to the `functionName` within the body of the function.<br><br>Methods can accept parameters. Each parameter is specified by its type and a variable. The variable becomes the local variable for the method.<br><br>Note: A `procedure` can also be defined in Pascal. A `procedure` does not return a value, it can, however, return parameters if passed by reference. | Java does not have global functions. Functions are always part of a java class. In Java, functions are called either member functions or methods.<br><br>Syntax:<br><br>`returnType functionName([parameterList]) {`<br>`    statements`<br>`}`<br><br>`returnType` – return type of a method. It is always required. If a method does not return anything, use void.<br>`functionName` – is the name of the method.<br><br>Methods can accept parameters. Each parameter is specified by its type and a variable. The variable becomes the local variable for the method.<br><br>A `return` statement is used to return from the method or return a value from the method.<br><br>A `return` statement is optional in a method with return type void.<br><br>A `return` statement is required for a method with a return type other than void. |

## 30. Method (Function) with one Parameter and Return Value - Example

| FORTRAN | Visual Basic |
|---|---|
| A function `ICUBED` is defined which expects one parameter of the type `INTEGER` and returns the cube of the number.<br><br>```<br>PROGRAM FUN1PAR<br>DO I=1, 6<br>   WRITE(*,*) I,'^3 IS',ICUBED(I)<br>END DO<br>STOP<br>END<br>FUNCTION ICUBED(IX)<br>INTEGER IX<br>ICUBED = IX * IX * IX<br>RETURN<br>END<br>``` | A function `cubed` is defined which expects one parameter of the type `INTEGER` and returns the cube of the number.<br><br>```<br>Private Sub Command1_Click()<br>Dim i As Integer<br>For i = 1 To 6<br>   Print i & "^3 is " & cubed(i)<br>Next i<br>End Sub<br>Function cubed(x As Integer) As Integer<br>cubed = x * x * x<br>End Function<br>``` |
| The output of the program:<br><br>```<br>1^3 is 1<br>2^3 is 8<br>3^3 is 27<br>4^3 is 64<br>5^3 is 125<br>``` | The output of the program:<br><br>```<br>1^3 is 1<br>2^3 is 8<br>3^3 is 27<br>4^3 is 64<br>5^3 is 125<br>``` |

## Method (Function) with one Parameter and Return Value - Example

| C | Java |
|---|---|
| A function `cubed` is defined which expects one parameter of the type `int` and returns the cube of the number. | A method (member function) `cubed()` is defined which expects one parameter of the type `int` and returns the cube of the number. The `cubed` function is declared `static` because it is being called from a `static` method. |

C:
```c
#include <Stdio.h>
int cubed(int x)
{
    return x * x * x;
}
int main()
{
    int i, c;
    for (i = 1; i < 6; i ++)
    {
        c = cubed(i);
        printf("%d^3 is %d\n", i, c);
    }
    return 0;
}
```

Java:
```java
class Method1{
    public static void main(String args[]){
      for (int i=1; i<6; i++) {
         int c = cubed(i);
         System.out.println(i +"^3 is " + c);
      }
    }
    static int cubed(int x) {
      return x * x * x;
    }
}
```

The output of the program:

```
1^3 is 1
2^3 is 8
3^3 is 27
4^3 is 64
5^3 is 125
```

The output of the program:

```
1^3 is 1
2^3 is 8
3^3 is 27
4^3 is 64
5^3 is 125
```

## Method (Function) with one Parameter and Return Value - Example

### COBOL

```
       IDENTIFICATION DIVISION.
      *-----------------------------
       PROGRAM-ID. METHOD1P.
      *-----------------------------
      *  This program accepts integer
      *  number from console and calculates
      *  its cube by calling the sub-program 'CUBEP'.
      *-----------------------------
       ENVIRONMENT DIVISION.
       CONFIGURATION SECTION.
       DATA DIVISION.
       WORKING-STORAGE SECTION.
       01 ACCEPT-INPUT.
          05 ACCEPT-INTEGER-ARRAY   OCCURS 6 TIMES.
             10 ACCEPT-INTEGER-A    PIC 99.
       01 DISPLAY-LINE .
          05 DISPLAY-FILLER1        PIC X(20)
                VALUE "The cube of Integer ".
          05 P-display-integer      PIC Z9BB.
          05 DISPLAY-FILLER2        PIC X(04)
                VALUE " is " .
          05 P-DISPLAY-RESULT       PIC Z(7)9.
       01 LINKED-BUFFER.
          05 LINKED-INTEGER         PIC 9(02).
          05 LINKED-RESULT          PIC 9(08).

       01 W-CNT                     PIC 99 COMP VALUE 0.
      *-----------------------------
       PROCEDURE DIVISION.
      *-----------------------------
       0000-MAIN.
      *---------
           DISPLAY SPACES.
           DISPLAY "Pl enter 6 integer Numbers"
           ACCEPT ACCEPT-INPUT

           PERFORM CALL-CUBEP THRU CALL-CUBEP-EXIT
               VARYING W-CNT FROM 1 BY 1
               UNTIL W-CNT > 6.
           STOP RUN.
```

```
       0000-EXIT. EXIT.
       CALL-CUBEP.
           MOVE ACCEPT-INTEGER-A(W-CNT) TO LINKED-INTEGER
           MOVE ZEROS                   TO LINKED-RESULT
           CALL "CUBEP" USING LINKED-BUFFER
           MOVE LINKED-INTEGER    TO P-DISPLAY-INTEGER
           MOVE LINKED-RESULT     TO P-DISPLAY-RESULT
           DISPLAY SPACES
           DISPLAY DISPLAY-LINE.
       CALL-CUBEP-EXIT.    EXIT.

       IDENTIFICATION DIVISION.

       PROGRAM-ID.     CUBEP.
      *---------------------------------------------------------------*
      *    This program returns cube of a passed integer              *
      *****************************************************************
       ENVIRONMENT DIVISION.

       CONFIGURATION SECTION.
       INPUT-OUTPUT SECTION.
       DATA DIVISION.
       WORKING-STORAGE SECTION.
       77 WS-RESULT   PIC S9(8) COMP VALUE 0.
       $PAGE " L I N K A G E    S E C T I O N"
       LINKAGE SECTION.
       01  SUB-BUFFER .
           05 SUB-INTEGER            PIC 9(02).
           05 SUB-RESULT             PIC 9(08).
       PROCEDURE DIVISION
                          USING   SUB-BUFFER .
       A0000-MAIN .
           MOVE 0 TO WS-RESULT .
           COMPUTE WS-RESULT = SUB-INTEGER * SUB-INTEGER * SUB-INTEGER
           MOVE WS-RESULT TO SUB-RESULT .
           PERFORM A0000-EXIT.
       A0000-EXIT. GOBACK.
```

### The output of above program is:
```
Pl enter 6 integer Numbers
020304050611
The cube of Integer  2  is          8
The cube of Integer  3  is         27
The cube of Integer  4  is         64
The cube of Integer  5  is        125
The cube of Integer  6  is        216
The cube of Integer 11  is       1331
```

## Method (Function) with one Parameter and Return Value - Example

| PASCAL | Java |
|---|---|
| A function `cubed` is defined which expects one parameter of the type `Integer` and returns the cube of the number.<br><br>```pascal<br>program method1;<br>{$APPTYPE CONSOLE}<br>uses<br>  SysUtils;<br>function cubed(x : Integer) : Integer;<br>begin<br>  result := x * x * x;<br>end;<br>var<br>  i, c : Integer;<br>begin<br>  for i := 1 to 5 do<br>  begin<br>    c := cubed(i);<br>    Writeln(IntToStr(i) + '^3 is ' +<br>          IntToStr(c));<br>  end;<br>end.<br>``` | A method (member function) `cubed()` is defined which expects one parameter of the type `int` and returns the cube of the number. The `cubed` function is declared `static` because it is being called from a `static` method.<br><br>```java<br>class Method1{<br>    public static void main(String args[]){<br>        for (int i=1; i<6; i++) {<br>            int c = cubed(i);<br>            System.out.println(i +"^3 is " + c);<br>        }<br>    }<br>    static int cubed(int x) {<br>        return x * x * x;<br>    }<br>}<br>``` |
| The output of the program:<br><br>```<br>1^3 is 1<br>2^3 is 8<br>3^3 is 27<br>4^3 is 64<br>5^3 is 125<br>``` | The output of the program:<br><br>```<br>1^3 is 1<br>2^3 is 8<br>3^3 is 27<br>4^3 is 64<br>5^3 is 125<br>``` |

## 31. Method (Function) with Two Parameters and Return Value - Example

| FORTRAN | Visual Basic |
|---|---|
| A function `MINIMUM` is defined which expects two parameters of the type `Integer` and returns the smaller of the two values.<br><br>```<br>      PROGRAM FUN1PAR<br>      INTEGER I, J<br>      I=12<br>      J=13<br>      WRITE(*,*) 'MINIMUM VALUE ',<br>     &            MINIMUM(I,J)<br>      STOP<br>      END<br>      FUNCTION MINIMUM(I1, I2)<br>      IF (I1 .LT. I2) THEN<br>         MINIMUM = I1<br>      ELSE<br>         MINIMUM = I2<br>      ENDIF<br>      RETURN<br>      END<br>``` | A function `Min` is defined which expects two parameters of the type `Integer` and returns the smaller of the two values.<br><br>```<br>Private Sub Command2_Click()<br>Dim i As Integer, j As Integer<br>i = 12<br>j = 13<br>Print "minimum value " & Min(i, j)<br>End Sub<br><br>Function Min(x As Integer, y As Integer) As Integer<br>If x < y Then<br>    Min = x<br>Else<br>    Min = y<br>End If<br>End Function<br>``` |
| The output of the program:<br><br>`MINIMUM VALUE 12` | The output of the program:<br><br>`minimum value 12` |

## Method (Function) with Two Parameters and Return Value - Example

| C | Java |
|---|---|
| A function `min()` is defined which expects two parameters of the type `int` and returns the smaller of the two values.<br><br>```c<br>#include <stdio.h><br>int min(int x, int y)<br>{<br>    if (x < y)<br>        return x;<br>    return y;<br>}<br><br>int main()<br>{<br>    int i = 12, j = 13;<br>    printf("minimum value %d\n", min(i,j));<br>    return 0;<br>}<br>``` | A method `min()` is defined which expects two parameters of the type `int` and returns the smaller of the two values.<br><br>```java<br>class Method2{<br>    public static void main(String args[]){<br>        int i=12, j = 13;<br>        System.out.println(<br>            "minimum value "+min(i,j));<br>    }<br>    static int min(int x, int y) {<br>        if (x < y) return x;<br>        return y;<br>    }<br>}<br>``` |
| The output of the program:<br><br>```<br>minimum value 12<br>``` | The output of the program:<br><br>```<br>minimum value 12<br>``` |

# Method (Function) with Two Parameters and Return Value - Example

## COBOL

```
        IDENTIFICATION DIVISION.
*-------------------------------
        PROGRAM-ID. METHOD2P.
*-------------------------------
*   This program accepts 2 integer
*   number from console and calls a
*   sub-program 'minP' to determine
*   minimum of two Integers.
*-------------------------------
        ENVIRONMENT DIVISION.
        CONFIGURATION SECTION.
        DATA DIVISION.
        WORKING-STORAGE SECTION.
        01 ACCEPT-INPUT.
           05 ACCEPT-INTEGER1    PIC 99.
           05 ACCEPT-INTEGER2    PIC 99.
        01 DISPLAY-LINE .
           05 DISPLAY-FILLER1    PIC X(32)
              VALUE "The Minimum of the two Integers ".
           05 P-INTEGER1         PIC Z9B.
           05 DISPLAY-FILLER2    PIC X(05)
              VALUE " and " .
           05 P-INTEGER2         PIC Z9.
           05 FILLER             PIC XXXX VALUE " is " .
           05 P-RESULT           PIC Z9.
        01 LINKED-BUFFER.
           05 LINKED-INTEGER1    PIC 9(02).
           05 LINKED-INTEGER2    PIC 9(02).
           05 LINKED-RESULT      PIC 9(02).
        01 W-CNT                 PIC 99 COMP VALUE 0.
```

```
*-------------------------------
        PROCEDURE DIVISION
        .
        0000-MAIN.
*---------
            DISPLAY SPACES.
            DISPLAY "Enter 2 integer Numbers"
            ACCEPT ACCEPT-INPUT
            PERFORM CALL-MINP   THRU CALL-MINP-EXIT.
            STOP RUN.
        0000-EXIT. EXIT.
        CALL-MINP.
            MOVE ACCEPT-INTEGER1   TO LINKED-INTEGER1
            MOVE ACCEPT-INTEGER2   TO LINKED-INTEGER2
            MOVE ZEROS             TO LINKED-RESULT
            CALL "MINP" USING LINKED-BUFFER
            MOVE LINKED-INTEGER1   TO P-INTEGER1
            MOVE LINKED-INTEGER2   TO P-INTEGER2
            MOVE LINKED-RESULT     TO P-RESULT
            DISPLAY SPACES
            DISPLAY DISPLAY-LINE .
        CALL-MINP-EXIT.   EXIT.
        IDENTIFICATION DIVISION.
        PROGRAM-ID.    MINP.
*   This program returns cube of a passed integer *
        ENVIRONMENT DIVISION.
        CONFIGURATION SECTION.
        INPUT-OUTPUT SECTION.
        DATA DIVISION.
        WORKING-STORAGE SECTION.
        77 WS-RESULT  PIC S9(2) COMP VALUE 0.
        $PAGE " L I N K A G E    S E C T I O N"

        LINKAGE SECTION.
        01  SUB-BUFFER .
            05 SUB-INTEGER1            PIC 9(02).
            05 SUB-INTEGER2            PIC 9(02).
            05 SUB-RESULT              PIC 9(02).
        PROCEDURE DIVISION
                       USING  SUB-BUFFER .
        A0000-MAIN .
            IF SUB-INTEGER1 < SUB-INTEGER2
                MOVE SUB-INTEGER1 TO SUB-RESULT
            ELSE
                MOVE SUB-INTEGER2 TO SUB-RESULT
            END-IF.
        A0000-EXIT. GOBACK.
```

The output of above program is:

```
Enter 2 integer Numbers
1107

The Minimum of the two Integers 11  and  7
is  7
```

## Method (Function) with Two Parameters and Return Value - Example

| PASCAL | Java |
|---|---|
| A function `min()` is defined which expects two parameters of the type `int` and returns the smaller of the two values. | A method `min()` is defined which expects two parameters of the type `int` and returns the smaller of the two values. |

PASCAL:
```
program method2;
{$APPTYPE CONSOLE}
uses
  SysUtils;
function min(x, y : Integer) : Integer;
begin
  if (x<y) then result := x else result := y;
end;
var
  i, j : Integer;
begin
  i := 12; j:= 13;
  Writeln('Minimum value ' +
IntToStr(min(i,j)));
end.
```

Java:
```
class Method2{
    public static void main(String args[]){
        int i=12, j = 13;
        System.out.println(
            "minimum value "+min(i,j));
    }
    static int min(int x, int y) {
        if (x < y) return x;
        return y;
    }
},
```

The output of the program:

PASCAL: `Minimum value 12`

Java: `minimum value 12`

## 32. Built-in Math Functions

| FORTRAN | Visual Basic |
|---|---|
| `abs(x)` – absolute value of x | `abs(x)` – absolute value of x |
| `sin(x)` – sine of x (radians) | `sin(x)` – sine of x (radians) |
| `cos(x)` – cosine of x (radians) | `cos(x)` – cosine of x (radians) |
| `tan(x)` – tangent of x (radians) | `tan(x)` – tangent of x (radians) |
| `asin(x)` – inverse sine of x | |
| `acos(x)` – inverse cosine of x | |
| `atan(x)` – inverse tangent of x | `atn(x)` – inverse tangent of x |
| `exp(x)` – returns $e^x$, where e is base of the natural log | `exp(x)` – returns $e^x$, where e is base of the natural log |
| `log(x)` – logarithm of x to the base e | `log(x)` – logarithm of x to the base e |
| `sqrt(x)` – square root of x | `sqr(x)` – square root of x |
| `x ** y` – computes $x^y$ | `x ^ y` – computes $x^y$ |
| `max(x1,x2)` – bigger of x1, x2 | |
| `min(x1,x2)` – smaller of x1, x2 | |
| `Int(x)`, `Ifix(x)` – functions for truncating and rounding floating point numbers | `Int(x)`, `Fix(x)` – functions for truncating and rounding floating point numbers |
| | `round(x)` – function for truncating and rounding floating point numbers |

## Built-in Math Functions

| C | Java |
|---|---|
| `abs(x)` – absolute value of x | `Math.abs(x)` – absolute value of x |
| `sin(x)` – sine of x (radians) | `Math.sin(x)` – sine of x (radians) |
| `cos(x)` – cosine of x (radians) | `Math.cos(x)` – cosine of x (radians) |
| `tan(x)` – tangent of x (radians) | `Math.tan(x)` – tangent of x (radians) |
| `asin(x)` – inverse sine of x | `Math.asin(x)` – inverse sine of x |
| `acos(x)` – inverse cosine of x | `Math.acos(x)` – inverse cosine of x |
| `atan(x)` – inverse tangent of x | `Math.atan(x)` – inverse tangent of x |
| `exp(x)` – returns $e^x$, where e is base of the natural log | `Math.exp(x)` – returns $e^x$, where e is base of the natural log |
| `log(x)` – logarithm of x to the base e | `Math.log(x)` – logarithm of x to the base e |
| `sqrt(x)` – square root of x | `Math.sqrt(x)` – square root of x |
| `pow(x,y)` – computes $x^y$ | `Math.pow(x,y)` – computes $x^y$ |
| `max(x1,x2)` – bigger of x1, x2 | `Math.max(x1,x2)` – bigger of x1, x2 |
| `min(x1,x2)` – smaller of x1, x2 | `Math.min(x1,x2)` – smaller of x1, x2 |
| `ceil(x)` – returns the smallest (closest to negative infinity) `double` value that is not less than the argument and is equal to a mathematical integer | `Math.ceil(x)` – Returns the smallest (closest to negative infinity) `double` value that is not less than the argument and is equal to a mathematical integer. |
| `floor(x)` – returns the largest (closest to positive infinity) `double` value that is not greater than the argument and is equal to a mathematical integer | `Math.floor(x)` – Returns the largest (closest to positive infinity) `double` value that is not greater than the argument and is equal to a mathematical integer. |
| | `Math.round(x)` – Returns the closest `int` to the argument. |

**Built-in Math Functions**

## COBOL

| | |
|---|---|
| `abs(x)` | – absolute value of x |
| `sin(x)` | – sine of x (radians) |
| `cos(x)` | – cosine of x (radians) |
| `tan(x)` | – tangent of x (radians) |
| `asin(x)` | – inverse sine of x |
| `acos(x)` | – inverse cosine of x |
| `atan(x)` | – inverse tangent of x |
| `exp(x)` | – returns $e^x$, where e is base of the natural log |
| `log(x)` | – logarithm of x to the base e |
| `sqrt(x)` | – square root of x |
| `max(x1, x2, ..)` | – returns the biggest form the list of values |
| `min(x1, x2, ..)` | – returns the smallest form the list of values |

**Built-in Math Functions**

| PASCAL | Java |
|---|---|
| `abs(x)` – absolute value of x | `Math.abs(x)` – absolute value of x |
| `sin(x)` – sine of x (radians) | `Math.sin(x)` – sine of x (radians) |
| `cos(x)` – cosine of x (radians) | `Math.cos(x)` – cosine of x (radians) |
| `tan(x)` – tangent of x (radians) | `Math.tan(x)` – tangent of x (radians) |
| `asin(x)` – inverse sine of x | `Math.asin(x)` – inverse sine of x |
| `acos(x)` – inverse cosine of x | `Math.acos(x)` – inverse cosine of x |
| `atan(x)` – inverse tangent of x | `Math.atan(x)` – inverse tangent of x |
| `exp(x)` – returns $e^x$, where e is base of the natural log | `Math.exp(x)` – returns $e^x$, where e is base of the natural log |
| `log(x)` – logarithm of x to the base e | `Math.log(x)` – logarithm of x to the base e |
| `sqrt(x)` – square root of x | `Math.sqrt(x)` – square root of x |
| `power(x,y)` – computes $x^y$ | `Math.pow(x,y)` – computes $x^y$ |
| `max(x1,x2)` – bigger of x1, x2 | `Math.max(x1,x2)` – bigger of x1, x2 |
| `min(x1,x2)` – smaller of x1, x2 | `Math.min(x1,x2)` – smaller of x1, x2 |
| `ceil(x)` – returns the smallest (closest to negative infinity) `double` value that is not less than the argument and is equal to a mathematical integer | `Math.ceil(x)` – Returns the smallest (closest to negative infinity) `double` value that is not less than the argument and is equal to a mathematical integer. |
| `floor(x)` – returns the largest (closest to positive infinity) `double` value that is not greater than the argument and is equal to a mathematical integer | `Math.floor(x)` – Returns the largest (closest to positive infinity) `double` value that is not greater than the argument and is equal to a mathematical integer. |
| `round(x)` – Returns the closest `int` to the argument. | `Math.round(x)` – Returns the closest `int` to the argument. |

## 33. Math Functions – Examples

| FORTRAN | Visual Basic |
|---|---|
| ```
PROGRAM MATH
REAL*4 A,B,C
A = 21.5
B = -64.3
C = 3.5
WRITE(*,*) SQRT(A)
WRITE(*,*) LOG(A)
WRITE(*,*) EXP(C)
WRITE(*,*) INT(A)
WRITE(*,*) IFIX(A)
WRITE(*,*) INT(B)
WRITE(*,*) IFIX(B)
STOP
END
``` | ```
Private Sub Command1_Click()
Dim a As Double
Dim b As Double
Dim c As Double
a = 21.5
b = -64.3
c = 3.5
Print Sqr(a)
Print (Log(a))
Print Exp(c)
Print Int(a)
Print Fix(a)
Print Round(a)
Print Round(b)
End Sub
``` |
| The output of the program:<br><br>   4.636809<br>   3.068053<br>  33.115450<br>       21<br>       21<br>      -64<br>      -64 | The output of the program:<br><br>4.63680924774785<br> 3.06805293513362<br> 33.1154519586923<br> 21<br> 21<br> 22<br>-64 |

## Math Functions – Examples

| C | Java |
|---|---|
| ```c
#include <stdio.h>
#include <math.h>

int main()
{
    double a = 21.5, b = -64.3, c = 3.5;
    printf("%lf\n", sqrt(a));
    printf("%lf\n", log(a));
    printf("%lf\n", exp(c));
    printf("%lf\n", ceil(a));
    printf("%lf\n", ceil(b));
    printf("%lf\n", floor(a));
    printf("%lf\n", floor(b));
    return 0;
}
``` | ```java
class MathFunctions{
    public static void main(String args[]){
    double a=21.5, b =-64.3, c = 3.5;

    System.out.println(Math.sqrt(a));
    System.out.println(Math.log(a));
    System.out.println(Math.exp(c));
    System.out.println(Math.ceil(a));
    System.out.println(Math.ceil(b));
    System.out.println(Math.floor(a));
    System.out.println(Math.floor(b));
    System.out.println(Math.round(a));
    System.out.println(Math.round(b));
    }
}
``` |
| The output of the program:<br><br>4.636809<br>3.068053<br>33.115452<br>22.000000<br>-64.000000<br>21.000000<br>-65.000000 | The output of the program:<br><br>4.636809247747852<br>3.068052935133617<br>33.11545195869231<br>22.0<br>-64.0<br>21.0<br>-65.0<br>22<br>-64 |

## Math Functions – Examples

### COBOL

```
        IDENTIFICATION DIVISION.
       *-----------------------------
        PROGRAM-ID. MATHFUNP.
       *  This program calls the standard
       *  math functions.
       *-----------------------------
        ENVIRONMENT DIVISION.
        CONFIGURATION SECTION.

        DATA DIVISION.

        WORKING-STORAGE SECTION.

        01 WS-NUM-LOG      PIC S9(2)V9(5) VALUE ZEROS.
        01 WS-NUM-LOG10    PIC S9(2)V9(5) VALUE ZEROS.
        01 WS-INT          PIC 99 VALUE 43.
        01 WS-SQUARE-ROOT  PIC S9(3)V9(3) VALUE ZEROS.

        PROCEDURE DIVISION
```

```
        0000-MAIN.
       *--------
        DISPLAY SPACES.
        COMPUTE WS-NUM-LOG = FUNCTION LOG (10).
        DISPLAY "LOG = ", WS-NUM-LOG
        COMPUTE WS-NUM-LOG10 = FUNCTION LOG10 (50).
        DISPLAY "LOG(Base 10) = " WS-NUM-LOG10.
        COMPUTE WS-SQUARE-ROOT = FUNCTION SQRT (64).
        DISPLAY "Square Root of 64 = ", WS-SQUARE-ROOT
        COMPUTE WS-SQUARE-ROOT = FUNCTION SQRT (WS-INT).
        DISPLAY "Square Root of 43 = ", WS-SQUARE-ROOT
        STOP RUN.
```

The output of the program :

```
LOG = +02.30258
LOG(Base 10) = +01.69897
Square Root of 64 = +008.000
Square Root of 43 = +006.557
```

## Math Functions – Examples

| PASCAL | Java |
|---|---|
| ```pascal
program MathFuntions;
{$APPTYPE CONSOLE}
uses
   SysUtils, Math;
var
   a, b, c : double;
begin
   a := 21.5; b := -64.3; c := 3.5;

   Writeln(sqrt(a));
   Writeln(log2(a));
   Writeln(exp(c));
   Writeln(ceil(a));
   Writeln(ceil(b));
   Writeln(floor(a));
   Writeln(floor(b));
   Writeln(round(a));
   Writeln(round(b));
end.
``` | ```java
class MathFunctions{
    public static void main(String args[]){
    double a=21.5, b =-64.3, c = 3.5;

    System.out.println(Math.sqrt(a));
    System.out.println(Math.log(a));
    System.out.println(Math.exp(c));
    System.out.println(Math.ceil(a));
    System.out.println(Math.ceil(b));
    System.out.println(Math.floor(a));
    System.out.println(Math.floor(b));
    System.out.println(Math.round(a));
    System.out.println(Math.round(b));
    }
}
``` |

| The output of the program: | The output of the program: |
|---|---|
| 4.63680924774785E+0000<br>4.42626475470210E+0000<br>3.31154519586923E+0001<br>22<br>-64<br>21<br>-65<br>22<br>-64 | 4.636809247747852<br>3.068052935133617<br>33.11545195869231<br>22.0<br>-64.0<br>21.0<br>-65.0<br>22<br>-64 |

## 34. Converting Strings to Numeric Types

| FORTRAN | Visual Basic |
|---|---|
| ```
CHARACTER*10 X
INTEGER D
X='123'
READ(X,'(I3)') D
WRITE(*,*) D
STOP
END
``` | In the following examples, the variable x is String type.<br><br>```
Dim x As String
x = "-999.35"
Dim a As Single, b As Double
Dim d As Integer, c As Long
Dim f As Byte

a = CDbl(x)
b = CSng(x)
d = CInt(x)
c = CLng(x)
f = CByte(x)
Print a, b, c, d, f
``` |

## Converting Strings to Numeric Types

| C | Java |
|---|---|
| ```c
#include <stdio.h>
#include <stdlib.h>
int main()
{
    char *a = "10";
    char *b = "14506950";
    char *f = "1.23";
    char *x = "1.032327";
    printf("Integer value of a is %d\n",
           atoi(a));
    printf("Long value of b is %ld\n",
           atol(b));
    printf("float value of f is %f\n",
           atof(f));
    printf("double value of x is %lf\n",
           strtod(x, (char **)NULL));
    return 0;
}
``` | In the following examples, the variable x is String type.<br><br>```java
double a = Double.parseDouble(x);
float b = Float.parseFloat(x);
long c = Long.parseLong(x);
int d = Integer.parseInt(x);
short e = Short.parseShort(x);
byte f = Byte.parseByte(x);
``` |

## Converting Strings to Numeric Types

### COBOL

Cobol is not a strongly typed language. In Cobol, the type of a group-item is always alpha-numeric. However, an elementary data-item exhibits the type as determined by its `picture` clause. There are no special functions in Cobol to change the data type of a variable.

Example:

```
01 SAMPLE-FIELD
   05    FIELD-X    PIC X(2).
   05    FIELD-N    PIC 99V99.
   MOVE "ABCXYZ" TO SAMPLE-FIELD

* The SAMPLE-FIELD  will now contain "CDEF".
```

## Converting Strings to Numeric Types

| PASCAL | Java |
|---|---|
| ```pascal
program MathFuntions;
{$APPTYPE CONSOLE}
uses
  SysUtils, Math;
var
  a : double;
  b : single;
  c : int64;
  d : integer;
  e : SmallInt;
  f : byte;
  x : string;
begin
  x := '21.5';
  a := StrToFloat(x);
  b := StrToFloat(x);
  c := StrToInt(x);
  d := StrToInt(x);
  e := StrToInt(x);
  f := StrToInt(x);
end.
``` | In the following examples, the variable x is String type.<br><br>```java
double a = Double.parseDouble(x);
float b = Float.parseFloat(x);
long c = Long.parseLong(x);
int d = Integer.parseInt(x);
short e = Short.parseShort(x);
byte f = Byte.parseByte(x);
``` |

## 35. String Operations - Returning a Substring

| FORTRAN | Visual Basic |
|---|---|
| A part of a string (character type variable) can be returned by using the indexes separated by :<br><br>`subStr = str(begin:end)`<br><br>Returns a string beginning at the `begin` character and ending with the `end` character.<br><br>Indexes start at one. | `Mid` function<br><br>`Mid(str, start, length)` – returns `length` number of characters starting at `start` from the string `str` |
| ``` PROGRAM SUBSTRING CHARACTER*25 S1 S1='Hello world Goodbye World' WRITE(*,*) S1(7:11) STOP END ``` | ``` Dim s1 As String s1 = "Hello World Goodbye World" Print Mid(s1, 7, 5) ``` |
| The output of the following program:<br><br>`World` | The output of the following program:<br><br>`World` |

## String Operations - Returning a Substring

| C | Java |
|---|---|
| Strings are treated as an array of characters. A substring can be accessed by using indexes. String indexes are zero-based. | *substring* method for the String class.<br><br>*substring(int beginIndex, int endIndex)* – returns part of the string starting with *beginIndex* and ending with *endIndex-1*. |
| ```#include <stdio.h>```<br>`#include <stdio.h>`<br>`#include <string.h>`<br>`int main()`<br>`{`<br>`    char *s1 = "Hello World Goodbye World";`<br>`    char s2[6];`<br>`    int i;`<br>`    for (i = 0; i < 6; i++)`<br>`        s2[i] = s1[i+6];`<br>`    s2[i] = '\0';`<br>`    printf("%s\n", s2);`<br>`    return 0;`<br>`}` | `class StringSub {`<br>`    public static void main (String args[]){`<br>`        String s1="Hello World Goodbye World";`<br>`        System.out.println(s1.substring(6,11));`<br>`    }`<br>`}` |
| The output of the following program:<br><br>`World` | The output of the following program:<br><br>`World` |

139

## String Operations - Returning a Substring

### COBOL

```
01 WS-STRING                 pic x(40)
    VALUE "Hello World Goodbye World".
01 WS-DISPLAY-STRING .
   05 CHAR-A PIC X OCCURS 40 TIMES.

01 BEGININDEX               PIC S99 COMP VALUE 0.
01 ENDINDEX                 PIC S99 COMP VALUE 0.
01 WS-IND                   PIC S99 COMP VALUE +1.
.
.
.
PROCEDURE DIVISION.
.
.
.
MOVE SPACES TO WS-DISPLAY-STRING.
MOVE 7 TO BEGININDEX.
MOVE 12 TO ENDINDEX.
PERFORM MOVE-CHAR VARYING BEGININDEX FROM 7 BY 1
        UNTIL BEGININDEX > ENDINDEX.
DISPLAY SPACES .
DISPLAY WS-DISPLAY-STRING.
STOP RUN.

MOVE-CHAR.
MOVE WS-STRING(BEGININDEX) TO CHAR-A(WS-IND).
ADD 1 TO WS-IND.
```

The output of the program:

```
world
```

## String Operations - Returning a Substring

| PASCAL | Java |
|---|---|
| `function Copy(S; Index, Count: Integer): string;`<br><br>`Copy` returns a string or array containing Count characters or elements starting at `S[Index]`. | *substring* method for the String class<br><br>*substring(int beginIndex, int endIndex)* – returns part of the string starting with *beginIndex* and ending with *endIndex-1*. |
| <pre>program StringSub;<br>{$APPTYPE CONSOLE}<br>var<br>  s1 : string;<br>begin<br>  s1 := 'Hello World Goodbye World';<br>  Writeln(copy(s1,7,5));<br>end.</pre> | <pre>class StringSub {<br>    public static void main (String args[]){<br>        String s1="Hello World Goodbye World";<br>        System.out.println(s1.substring(6,11));<br>    }<br>}</pre> |
| The output of the following program:<br><br>`World` | The output of the following program:<br><br>`World` |

# 36. String Operations – Searching within a String for a Sequence of Characters

| FORTRAN | Visual Basic |
|---|---|
| `Index` function<br><br>`Index(str1,str2)` – returns the starting position of *str2* in *str1*.<br><br>Index of the first character is one. | `InStr` function<br><br>`InStr(str1,str2)` – returns the starting position of *str2* in *str1*.<br><br>Index of the first character is one. |
| ```<br>PROGRAM INDEXSTR<br>CHARACTER*25 S1<br>S1='Hello world Goodbye World'<br>WRITE(*,*) INDEX(S1,'Good')<br>STOP<br>END<br>``` | ```<br>Dim s1 As String<br>s1 = "Hello World Goodbye World"<br>Print InStr(s1, "Good")<br>``` |
| The output of the following program:<br><br>13 | The output of the following program:<br><br>13 |

## String Operations – Searching within a String for a Sequence of Characters

| C | Java |
|---|---|
| strstr function<br><br>strstr(str1,str2) – returns the starting position of str2 in str1.<br><br>Index of the first character is zero. | indexOf method for the String class<br><br>indexOf(String str) – returns index within this string of the first occurrence of the specified substring.<br><br>Index of the first character is zero. |
| <pre>#include <string.h><br>#include <stdio.h><br>int main()<br>{<br>    char *s1 = "Hello World Goodbye World";<br>    char *l;<br>    int len;<br>    l = strstr(s1, "Good");<br>    len = l - s1;<br>    printf("%d\n", len);<br>    return 0;<br>}</pre> | <pre>class StringSearch {<br>    public static void main (String args[]){<br>        String s1="Hello World Goodbye World";<br>        System.out.println(s1.indexOf("Good"));<br>    }<br>}</pre> |
| The output of the following program:<br><br>12 | The output of the following program:<br><br>12 |

## String Operations – Searching within a String for a Sequence of Characters

### COBOL

```
        IDENTIFICATION DIVISION.
        PROGRAM-ID. STRP.
      * This program returns the starting postion
      * of a substring in string.

        ENVIRONMENT DIVISION.
        CONFIGURATION SECTION.
        DATA DIVISION.

        WORKING-STORAGE SECTION.
        01 WS-STRING              PIC x(40)
           VALUE "HELLO WORLD GOODBYE WORLD".
        01 FILLER   REDEFINES WS-STRING .
           05 STR-X            PIC X OCCURS 40.
        01 WS-SUBSTRING      PIC X(04) VALUE "GOOD".
        01 FILLER REDEFINES    WS-SUBSTRING .
           05 SUBSTR-X         PIC X OCCURS 4 .
        01 DISPLAY-LINE .
           05 P-DISPLAY-RESULT PIC 99 .
        01 WS-IND            PIC S99 COMP VALUE ZERO.
        01 WS-CNT            PIC S99 COMP VALUE ZERO.
        01 WS-STARTING-POS   PIC 99 VALUE ZEROS.
        01 STRING-FOUND-FLAG PIC X VALUE SPACES.

        PROCEDURE DIVISION.
```

```
        0000-MAIN.
       *---------

           DISPLAY SPACES.
           PERFORM FIND-SUBSTR THRU FIND-SUBSTR-EXIT
               VARYING WS-IND FROM 1 BY 1
               UNTIL WS-IND  > 40
           MOVE 1 TO WS-CNT
           DISPLAY WS-STARTING-POS.
           STOP RUN.
        0000-EXIT. EXIT.
        FIND-SUBSTR.
           IF STR-X (WS-IND)      = SUBSTR-X(WS-CNT)
              MOVE WS-IND TO WS-STARTING-POS
              MOVE "Y"    TO STRING-FOUND-FLAG
              PERFORM CHK-STR VARYING WS-CNT FROM 1 BY 1
                 UNTIL WS-CNT > 4
              IF STRING-FOUND-FLAG EQUAL SPACES
                 MOVE WS-STARTING-POS TO WS-IND
                 MOVE 1 TO WS-CNT.
        FIND-SUBSTR-EXIT.   EXIT.
        CHK-STR.
           IF STR-X (WS-IND) <> SUBSTR-X(WS-CNT)
              MOVE SPACES TO STRING-FOUND-FLAG.
           ADD 1 TO WS-IND.
```

The output of above program:

13

## String Operations – Searching within a String for a Sequence of Characters

| PASCAL | Java |
|---|---|
| `POS` function<br><br>`strstr(str1,str2)` – returns the starting position of `str1` in `str2`.<br><br>Index of the first character is one. | `indexOf` method for the String class<br><br>`indexOf(String str)` – returns index within this string of the first occurrence of the specified substring.<br><br>Index of the first character is zero. |
| ```pascal<br>program StringSearch;<br>{$APPTYPE CONSOLE}<br>var<br>  s1 : string;<br>begin<br>  s1 := 'Hello World Goodbye World';<br>  Writeln(POS('Good',s1));<br>end.<br>``` | ```java<br>class StringSearch {<br>    public static void main (String args[]){<br>        String s1="Hello World Goodbye World";<br>        System.out.println(s1.indexOf("Good"));<br>    }<br>}<br>``` |
| The output of the following program:<br><br>13 | The output of the following program:<br><br>12 |

## 37. String Operations -- Replacing Character within a String with a new Character

| FORTRAN | Visual Basic |
|---|---|
| A character within a string can be replaced directly by specifying the location.<br><br>`str(L:L) = newCh`<br><br>Replaces the character at position L with a `newCh` character. | `Mid` function<br><br>`Mid` function can be used to extract or replace characters within a string. |
| ```<br>PROGRAM SUBSTRING<br>CHARACTER*25 S1<br>S1='Hello world Goodbye World'<br>DO I=1,25<br>   IF (S1(I:I).EQ.'o') S1(I:I)='x'<br>END DO<br>WRITE(*,*) S1<br>STOP<br>END<br>``` | ```<br>Dim I As Integer<br>Dim s1 As String * 25<br>s1 = "Hello World Goodbye World"<br>For I = 1 To 25<br>   If Mid(s1, I, 1) = "o" Then<br>      Mid(s1, I, 1) = "x"<br>   End If<br>Next I<br>Print s1<br>``` |
| The output of the above program:<br><br>`Hellx Wxrld Gxxdbye Wxrld` | The output of the above program:<br><br>`Hellx Wxrld Gxxdbye Wxrld` |

## String Operations -- Replacing Character within a String with a new Character

| C | Java |
|---|---|
| Strings are treated as an array of characters. An individual character can be replaced as in any array. | *replace* method of the `String` class.<br><br>*replace(char oldChar, char newChar)* – replaces all occurrences of *oldChar* in this string with *newChar*. |

<table>
<tr><td>

```c
#include <stdio.h>
#include <malloc.h>
#include <string.h>
int main()
{
    char *s1 = "Hello World Goodbye World";
    int i;
    char *s2 = (char *) malloc(((strlen(s1)) + 1) * sizeof(char));
    strcpy(s2, s1);
    for (i = 0; i < strlen(s1); i++)
        if (s1[i] == 'o')
            s2[i] = 'x';
    printf("%s\n", s2);
    free(s2);
    return 0;
}
```

</td><td>

```java
class StringReplace {
    public static void main (String args[]){
        String s1="Hello World Goodbye World";
        s1 = s1.replace('o','x');
        System.out.println(s1);
    }
}
```

</td></tr>
<tr><td>

The output of the above program:

Hellx Wxrld Gxxdbye Wxrld

</td><td>

The output of the above program:

Hellx Wxrld Gxxdbye Wxrld

</td></tr>
</table>

## String Operations -- Replacing Character within a String with a new Character

### COBOL

Use `INSPECT …. REPLACING` construct to replace selected characters within a string.

```
        IDENTIFICATION DIVISION.
       *--------------------------
        PROGRAM-ID. METHOD2P.
       *--------------------------
       *  This program replaces all occurrences of
       *  a character with a new Character
       *--------------------------
        ENVIRONMENT DIVISION.
        CONFIGURATION SECTION.
        DATA DIVISION.
        WORKING-STORAGE SECTION.
        01 WS-STRING                PIC X(40) VALUE
            "HELLO WORLD GOODBYE WORLD".
       *--------------------------
        PROCEDURE DIVISION      .
       *--------------------------
        0000-MAIN.
       *---------
            DISPLAY SPACES.
          INSPECT WS-STRING REPLACING ALL "O" BY "X".
            DISPLAY WS-STRING.
        0000-EXIT. EXIT.
```

The output of the program:

HELLX WXRLD GXXDBYE WXRLD

148

## String Operations -- Replacing Character within a String with a new Character

| PASCAL | Java |
|---|---|
| *function* `StringReplace(const S, OldPattern, NewPattern: string; Flags: TReplaceFlags): string;`<br><br>`StringReplace` replaces occurrences of one substring, specified by `OldPattern`, with another substring, specified by `NewPattern`, in a given string. `StringReplace` assumes the string may contain Multibyte characters.<br><br>If the Flags parameter does not include `rfReplaceAll`, `StringReplace` only replaces the first occurrence of `OldPattern` in the string S. If the Flags parameter includes `rfIgnoreCase`, The string comparison operation is case insensitive. | `replace` method of the `String` class.<br><br>`replace(char oldChar, char newChar)` – replaces all occurrences of `oldChar` in this string with `newChar`. |
| ```
program ReplaceString;
{$APPTYPE CONSOLE}
uses
  SysUtils;
var
  s1, s2 : string;
begin
  s1 := 'Hello World Goodbye World';
  s2 := StringReplace(s1,'o','x',[rfReplaceAll]);
  Writeln(s2);
end.
``` | ```
class StringReplace {
    public static void main (String args[]){
        String s1="Hello World Goodbye World";
        s1 = s1.replace('o','x');
        System.out.println(s1);
    }
}
``` |
| The output of the above program:<br><br>`Hellx Wxrld Gxxdbye Wxrld` | The output of the above program:<br><br>`Hellx Wxrld Gxxdbye Wxrld` |

## 38. Date and Time Functions

| FORTRAN | Visual Basic |
|---|---|
| The following subroutines can be used for getting or setting the system date and time:<br><br>`GETTIM(IH, IMIN, IS, IHUN)` - returns system time<br>`GETDAT(IY, IMON, ID)` - returns system date<br>`SETTIM(IH, IMIN, IS, IHUN)` - sets the system time<br>`SETDAT(IY, IMON, ID)` - sets the system date<br><br>where<br><br>  `IH` – hours (0 to 23)<br>  `IMIN` – minutes (0 to 59)<br>  `IS` – seconds (0 to 59)<br>  `IHUN` – hundredth of seconds (0 to 100)<br>  `IY` – years<br>  `IMON` – month number (1 to 12)<br>  `ID` – day number (1 to 31) | The following functions are available to extract values from a variable of the type Date<br><br>`Month(d)` – returns month number (1 to 12)<br>`Year(d)` – returns year (4 digits)<br>`Day(d)` – returns day (1 to 31)<br>`Hour(d)` – returns hours (0 to 23)<br>`Minute(d)` – returns minutes (0 to 59)<br>`Seconds(d)` – returns seconds (0 to 59)<br><br>`d` is any valid date |

## Date and Time Functions

| C | Java |
|---|---|
| There is a structure called time_t defined in `time.h` file. This has variables like `day, month, year, hour, min, sec` etc.<br><br>To set the time, use `mktime()` function.<br><br>The time and date functions in C are system dependent. | Time and date functions require an object of the type `GregorianCalendar`. The following statement creates and object variable `gc` of the type `GregorianCalendar` which now contains the time and the date at which the object was created.<br>`GregorianCalendar gc = `<br>`                new GregorianCalendar();`<br><br>To extract year, month, date, hour, minute, second values stored in the object, use the following methods:<br><br>`get(Calendar.MONTH)` – returns month (0 to 11)<br>`get(Calendar.DATE)` – returns date (1 to 31)<br>`get(Calendar.YEAR)` – returns year in 4 digits<br>`get(Calendar.HOUR)` – returns hour (0 to 23)<br>`get(Calendar.MINUTE)` – returns minute (0 to 59)<br>`get(Calendar.SECOND)` – returns seconds (0 to 59)<br><br>User-defined date/time object can be created using the following methods (values are set to `i`)<br><br>`gc.set(Calendar.MONTH,i);`<br>`gc.set(Calendar.YEAR,i);`<br>`gc.set(Calendar.DATE,i);`<br>`gc.set(Calendar.HOUR,i);`<br>`gc.set(Calendar.MINUTE,i);`<br>`gc.set(Calendar.SECOND,i);` |

### Date and Time Functions

**COBOL**

Function CURRENT-DATE contains information regarding the system date and time. The date/time functions are operating system dependent.

## Date and Time Functions

| PASCAL | Java |
|---|---|
| Most of the Date and Time functions can be handled through the classes `TDateTime` and `TTimeStamp`.<br><br>Working with `TDateTime`:<br><br>To extract year, month, date, hour, minute, second values stored in the `TDateTime` type, use the following functions:<br>`DecodeDate` breaks `TDateTime` into Year, Month, and Day values.<br>   *procedure DecodeDate(Date: TDateTime; var Year, Month, Day: Word);*<br>`DecodeTime` breaks `TDateTime` into hours, minutes, seconds, and milliseconds.<br>   *procedure DecodeTime(Time: TDateTime; var Hour, Min, Sec, MSec: Word);*<br><br>To set the values uses these procedures.<br><br>`EncodeDate` returns a `TDateTime` type for a specified Year, Month, and Day.<br>   *function EncodeDate(Year, Month, Day: Word): TDateTime;*<br>`EncodeTime` returns a `TDateTime` type for a specified Hour, Min, Sec, and MSec.<br>   *function EncodeTime(Hour, Min, Sec, MSec: Word): TDateTime;* | Time and date functions require an object of the type `GregorianCalendar`. The following statement creates and object variable `gc` of the type `GregorianCalendar` which now contains the time and the date at which the object was created.<br>`GregorianCalendar gc =`<br>                   `new GregorianCalendar();`<br><br>To extract year, month, date, hour, minute, second values stored in the object, use the following methods:<br><br>*get(Calendar.MONTH)* – returns month (0 to 11)<br>*get(Calendar.DATE)* – returns date (1 to 31)<br>*get(Calendar.YEAR)* – returns year in 4 digits<br>*get(Calendar.HOUR)* – returns hour (0 to 23)<br>*get(Calendar.MINUTE)* – returns minute (0 to 59)<br>*get(Calendar.SECOND)* – returns seconds (0 to 59)<br><br>User-defined date/time object can be created using the following methods (values are set to `i`):<br><br>*gc.set(Calendar.MONTH,i);*<br>*gc.set(Calendar.YEAR,i);*<br>*gc.set(Calendar.DATE,i);*<br>*gc.set(Calendar.HOUR,i);*<br>*gc.set(Calendar.MINUTE,i);*<br>*gc.set(Calendar.SECOND,i);* |

## 39. Date and Time Functions - Example

| FORTRAN | Visual Basic |
|---|---|
| ```
INTEGER*2 IHOUR, IMIN, ISEC, IHUN
INTEGER*2 IYEAR, IMONTH, IDAY
CALL GETTIM(IHOUR, IMIN, ISEC, IHUN )
CALL GETDAT(IYEAR, IMONTH, IDAY)
WRITE(*,*) IHOUR, IMIN, ISEC
WRITE(*,*) IYEAR, IMONTH, IDAY
STOP
END
``` | ```
Private Sub Command1_Click()
Dim today
Dim OtherDay
' today's date
today = Now
Print Month(today)
Print Year(today)
Print Day(today)
Print Hour(today)
Print Minute(today)
Print Second(today)
Print today
' create a user-defined date
OtherDay = #2/1/1989 3:30:10 PM#
Print OtherDay
End Sub
``` |
| The output of the program:<br><br>    10           15           25<br>  2000           2           19 | The output of the program:<br><br>2<br> 2000<br> 19<br> 10<br> 14<br> 36<br>2/19/00 10:14:36 AM<br>2/1/89 3:30:10 PM |

## Date and Time Functions -- Example

### C

```c
#include <stdio.h>

#include <time.h>
int main()
{
    struct tm when;
    time_t now;
    time(&now);
    when = *localtime(&now);
    printf("Date and Time are: %s\n",
asctime(&when));
    when.tm_mday = 29;
    when.tm_mon = 11;
    when.tm_year = 98;
    when.tm_hour = 10;
    when.tm_min = 30;
    when.tm_sec = 15;
    mktime(&when);
    printf(
      "User-defined date and time are: %s\n",
       asctime(&when));
    return 0;
}
```

### Java

```java
import java.util.*;

class GCDemo {
  public static void main(String args[]) {
    int year;
      //create a date/time object using the current
      //system time and date
    GregorianCalendar gc = new GregorianCalendar();
    System.out.print("Date: ");
    System.out.print(gc.get(Calendar.MONTH)+1);
    System.out.print(" " +gc.get(Calendar.DATE)+" ");
    System.out.println(year = gc.get(Calendar.YEAR));

    System.out.print("Time: ");
    System.out.print(gc.get(Calendar.HOUR) + ":");
    System.out.print(gc.get(Calendar.MINUTE) + ":");
    System.out.println(gc.get(Calendar.SECOND));
      //Create an user-defined date/time object
      gc.set(Calendar.MONTH,11);
      gc.set(Calendar.YEAR,1998);
      gc.set(Calendar.DATE,28);
      gc.set(Calendar.HOUR,22);
      gc.set(Calendar.MINUTE,30);
      gc.set(Calendar.SECOND,15);
    System.out.print("User-defined date ");
    System.out.print(gc.get(Calendar.MONTH)+1);
    System.out.print(" " +c.get(Calendar.DATE)+ " ");
    System.out.println(year = gc.get(Calendar.YEAR));

    System.out.print("and time: ");
    System.out.print(gc.get(Calendar.HOUR) + ":");
    System.out.print(gc.get(Calendar.MINUTE) + ":");
    System.out.println(gc.get(Calendar.SECOND));
  }
}
```

## Date and Time Functions -- Example

### COBOL

```cobol
            IDENTIFICATION DIVISION.
*---------------------------
            PROGRAM-ID. DTDEMOP.
*---------------------------
*   This program show time & date functions.
*---------------------------
            ENVIRONMENT DIVISION.
            CONFIGURATION SECTION.
            DATA DIVISION.
            WORKING-STORAGE SECTION.
            01 FULL-CURRENT-DATE  .
               05 C-DATE.
                  10 C-YEAR        PIC 9(4).
                  10 C-MONTH       PIC 99.
                  10 C-DAY         PIC 99.
               05 C-TIME.
                  10 C-HOUR        PIC 99.
                  10 C-MINUTES     PIC 99.
                  10 C-SECONDS     PIC 99.
                  10 C-SEC-HUND    PIC 99.
               05 C-TIME-DIFF.
                  10 C-GMT-DIR     PIC X.
                  10 C-HOUR        PIC 99.
                  10 C-MINUTES     PIC 99.
```

```cobol
*---------------------------
            PROCEDURE DIVISION
            .
*---------------------------
            0000-MAIN.
*---------
               DISPLAY SPACES.
               MOVE FUNCTION CURRENT-DATE TO FULL-CURRENT-DATE.
               DISPLAY "Full date is:", FULL-CURRENT-DATE.
               DISPLAY "year is: ", C-YEAR.
               DISPLAY "Month is: ", C-MONTH.
               DISPLAY "Day is: ", C-DAY.
               DISPLAY "Hour is: ", C-HOUR OF C-TIME.
               DISPLAY "Minute is: ", C-MINUTES OF C-TIME.
               DISPLAY "Second is: ", C-SECONDS.
               DISPLAY "Hundredths of seconds is: ", C-SEC-HUND.
               DISPLAY "Difference from GMT is: ", C-GMT-DIR
               DISPLAY "Hours from GMT is: ", C-HOUR OF C-TIME-DIFF
               DISPLAY "Minutes from GMT is: ", C-MINUTES OF C-TIME-DIFF


            0000-EXIT. EXIT.
```

**The output of program:**

```
Full date is:2000020223185000-0800
year is: 2000
Month is: 02
Day is: 02
Hour is: 23
Minute is: 18
Second is: 50
Hundredths of seconds is: 00
Difference from GMT is: -
Hours from GMT is: 08
Minutes from GMT is: 00
```

## Date and Time Functions -- Example

### PASCAL

```pascal
program GCDemo;
{$APPTYPE CONSOLE}
uses
   SysUtils;
var
   year, month, date, hour, minute, second, msec : Word;
   gc   : TDateTime;
begin
// Initialize a Date-Time variable with the current
// system time and date.
   gc := NOW;   // Built-in function for current Date/Time

   Write('Date :');
   DecodeDate(gc,year, month, date);
   Write(month);
   Write(' ' + IntToStr(date) + ' ');
   Writeln(year);
   Write('Time :');
   DecodeTime(gc,hour, minute, second, msec);
   Write(IntToStr(hour) + ':');
   Write(IntToStr(minute) + ':');
   Writeln(second);
// Create a user-defined TDateTime variable
   month  := 11;
   year   := 1998;
   date   := 28;
   hour   := 22;
   minute := 30;
   second := 15;
   msec   := 0;
   gc := EncodeDate(year, month, date);
   gc := gc + EncodeTime(hour,minute,second,msec);
   Write('User-defined date: ');
   DecodeDate(gc,year, month, date);
   Write(month);
   Write(' ' + IntToStr(date) + ' ');
   Writeln(year);
   Write('Time :');
   DecodeTime(gc,hour, minute, second, msec);
   Write(IntToStr(hour) + ':');
   Write(IntToStr(minute) + ':');
   Writeln(second);
end.
```

### Java

```java
import java.util.*;

class GCDemo {
  public static void main(String args[]) {
    int year;
      //create a date/time object using the current
      //system time and date
    GregorianCalendar gc = new GregorianCalendar();
    System.out.print("Date: ");
    System.out.print(gc.get(Calendar.MONTH)+1);
    System.out.print(" " +gc.get(Calendar.DATE)+" ");
    System.out.println(year = gc.get(Calendar.YEAR));

    System.out.print("Time: ");
    System.out.print(gc.get(Calendar.HOUR) + ":");
    System.out.print(gc.get(Calendar.MINUTE) + ":");
    System.out.println(gc.get(Calendar.SECOND));
      //Create an user-defined date/time object
    gc.set(Calendar.MONTH,11);
    gc.set(Calendar.YEAR,1998);
    gc.set(Calendar.DATE,28);
    gc.set(Calendar.HOUR,22);
    gc.set(Calendar.MINUTE,30);
    gc.set(Calendar.SECOND,15);
    System.out.print("User-defined date ");
    System.out.print(gc.get(Calendar.MONTH)+1);
    System.out.print(" " +c.get(Calendar.DATE)+ " ");
    System.out.println(year = gc.get(Calendar.YEAR));

    System.out.print("and time: ");
    System.out.print(gc.get(Calendar.HOUR) + ":");
    System.out.print(gc.get(Calendar.MINUTE) + ":");
    System.out.println(gc.get(Calendar.SECOND));
  }
}
```

## 40. One Dimensional Arrays

| FORTRAN | Visual Basic |
|---|---|
| General form for declaring a dynamic array<br><br>`TYPE varName[ALLOCATABLE](:)`<br>`        declares an array of integers`<br>`ALLOCATE(vaName(size))  'allocates memory`<br>`                        ' for the array`<br><br>The following two lines create an array to hold 12 integer values.<br><br>`INTEGER DAYS[ALLOCATABLE](:)`<br>`ALLOCATE(DAYS(12))`<br><br>When an array is created, its elements are all initialized to their default types. For numeric types, the elements are all set to zeroes, for boolean types they are set to.<br>The lower bound for the index is 1 by default.<br><br>Once created, the arrays can be used as follows:<br><br>`days(3) = 31    'sets the value`<br>`Write(*,*) days(2)    'print value` | General form for declaring a dynamic array<br><br>`Dim varName() as Integer`<br>`            'declares an array of integers`<br>`Redim varName(ubound)  'allocates memory`<br>`                       ' for the array`<br><br>The following two lines create an array to hold 12 integer values.<br><br>`Dim days() as Integer`<br>`Redim days(11)`<br><br>When an array is created, its elements are all initialized to their default types. For numeric types, the elements are all set to zeroes, for boolean types they are set to false and for objects they are set to `Nothing`.<br>The lower bound for the index is zero by default, the size is then upper bound +1. The lower bound depends on the `Option Base` setting.<br><br>Once created, the arrays can be used as follows:<br><br>`days(3) = 31    'sets the value`<br>`Print days(2)    'print value` |

158

## One Dimensional Arrays

| C | Java |
|---|---|
| General form for declaring an array<br><br>`int varName[size]; //declares and`<br>`     //allocates memory for the array`<br><br>The following two line creates an array to hold 12 `int` values.<br><br>`int days[12];`<br><br>When an array is created, its elements are all initialized to unknown values. The lower bound for the index is always zero, the upper bound always size-1.<br><br>Once created, the arrays can be used as follows:<br><br>`days[3] = 31; //sets the value`<br>`printf("%d",days[2]) // print value` | General form for declaring an array<br><br>`type varName []; //declares an array`<br>`varName = new type[size]; //allocates memory`<br>`                         // for the array`<br><br>The following two lines create an array to hold 12 `int` values.<br><br>`int days[];`<br>`days = new int[12];`<br><br>or<br><br>`int days[] = new int[12];`<br><br>When an array is created, its elements are all initialized to their default types. For numeric types, the elements are all set to zeroes, for boolean types they are set to false and for objects they are set to null.<br>The lower bound for the index is always zero, the upper bound always size-1.<br><br>Once created, the arrays can be used as follows:<br><br>`days[3] = 31; //sets the value`<br>`System.out.println(days[2]) // print value` |

**One Dimensional Arrays**

## COBOL

General form for declaring an array:

```
01 Employee-info .
   05 Employee-name        pic x(40).
   05 Employee-monthly-income occurs 12 Times Pic s9(5)V9(2).
```

The `occurs 12 times` sets up a table in memory storage holding the conceptual monthly salary of the employee for 12 months. The lower bound for the array is always one and upper bound is equal to `occurs n times`.

Cobol does not initializes arrays at run-time. It's the programmer's responsibility to initialize the array in the program.

The individual members in the array can be referred as

```
   *   If the Employee-monthly-income in 3rd month is greater than 6000

       If Employee-monthly-income (3) > 6000   OR


   *   If the Employee-monthly-income(ws-index) Where ws-index is
   *   defined as pic s99

     If Employee-monthly-income (ws-index) > zeros
```

160

## One Dimensional Arrays

| PASCAL | Java |
|---|---|
| General form for declaring an array<br><br>`varName : array of type;// Declares an array`<br>`SetLength(varName, size); // allocates`<br>`              //memory for the array`<br><br>The following two lines create an array to hold 12 `int` values.<br><br>`days : array of int;`<br>`SetLength(days ,12);`<br><br>or<br><br>`days : array [0..11] of int;`<br><br>When an array is created, its elements are all initialized to their default types. For numeric types, the elements are all set to zero, for boolean types, they are set to false, and for objects, they are set to `nil`.<br>The lower bound for the index is set to zero for the SetLength method or the lower value specified for static arrays. The upper bound is size-1 for dynamic arrays and the specified value for static arrays.<br><br>Once created, the arrays can be used as follows:<br><br>`days[3] := 31;   // Sets the value`<br>`Writeln(days[2]); // Prints the value` | General form for declaring an array<br><br>`type varName []; //declares an array`<br>`varName = new type[size]; //allocates memory`<br>`                    // for the array`<br><br>The following two lines create an array to hold 12 `int` values.<br><br>`int days[];`<br>`days = new int[12];`<br><br>or<br><br>`int days[] = new int[12];`<br><br>When an array is created, its elements are all initialized to their default types. For numeric types, the elements are all set to zeroes, for boolean types they are set to false and for objects they are set to null.<br>The lower bound for the index is always zero, the upper bound always size-1.<br><br>Once created, the arrays can be used as follows:<br><br>`days[3] = 31; //sets the value`<br>`System.out.println(days[2]) // print value` |

## 41. Two Dimensional Arrays

| FORTRAN | Visual Basic |
|---|---|
| General form for declaring a two-dimensional dynamic array<br><br>`TYPE varName[ALLOCATABLE](: , :)`<br>            declares an array<br>`ALLOCATE(vaName(size1,size2))`<br>            'allocates memory<br>            ' for the array<br><br>The following two lines create an array of 3 rows and 4 columns:<br><br>`INTEGER TABLE[ALLOCATABLE](:,:)`<br>`ALLOCATE(TABLE(3,4))`<br><br>Once created, the arrays can be used as follows:<br><br>`TABLE(3,4) = 31`    'sets the value<br>`Write(*,*) TABLE(2,4)`    'print value | General form for declaring a two-dimensional dynamic array<br><br>`Dim varName() as Integer`<br>            'declares an array of integers<br>`Redim varName(ubound1,ubound2)`<br>            'allocates memory<br>            ' for the array<br><br>The following two lines create a 2-dimensional array to hold 120 integer values(10 by 12):<br><br>`Dim days() as Integer`<br>`Redim days(9, 11)`<br><br>Once created, the arrays can be used as follows:<br><br>`days(3 , 5) = 31`    'sets the value<br>`Print days(7, 8)`    'prints value |

162

## Two Dimensional Arrays

| C | Java |
|---|---|
| General form for declaring two-dimensional array<br><br>`type varName [size1][size2]; //declares an`<br>`//array allocates memory for the array`<br><br>The following two lines create an array of 3 rows and 4 columns to hold int values.<br><br>`int table[3][4];`<br><br>The indexes for the first dimension are from 0 to 2, for the second dimension from 0 to 3.<br><br>Examples:<br><br>`table[2][3]=23;`<br>`int y = table[1][3];` | General form for declaring two-dimensional array<br><br>`type varName [][]; //declares an array`<br>`varName = new type[size1][size2];`<br>`            //allocates memory for the array`<br><br>The following two lines create an array of 3 rows and 4 columns to hold int values.<br><br>`int table[][];`<br>`table = new int[3][4];`<br><br>or<br><br>`int table[] = new int[3][4];`<br><br>The valid indexes for the first dimension are from 0 to 2, for the second dimension from 0 to 3.<br><br>Examples:<br><br>`table[2][3]=23;`<br>`int y = table[1][3];` |

## Two Dimensional Arrays

### COBOL

The concept of dimension refers to categories by which data is organized within tables. Two-dimensional tables requires two subscripts to locate the individual entry or field.

Ex: Assume a particular company has 4 divisions and we desired to set up a sales-table that will contain the monthly sales data of each divisions.

```
In DATA DIVISION.
:
:
01 SALES-TABLE
     05 DIVISION-SALES    OCCURS 4 TIMES.
        10 MONTHLY-SALES OCCURS 12 TIMES.
           15 SALES       PIC S9(5)V9(2).
For a two-dimensional table we require 2 subscripts.

01  Division-index         pic 99.
01  monthly-index          pic 99.

In Procedure Division

PROCEDURE DIVISION.
:
PERFORM CALCULATE SALES-TOTAL VARYING DIVISION-INDEX
                         FROM 1 BY 1 UNTIL
DIVISION-INDEX > 4
                  AFTER MONTHLY-INDEX FROM 1 BY 1
                         UNTIL MONTHLY-INDEX > 12.
:
:
SALES-TOTAL.
      ADD SALES-TOTAL (Division-index,MONTHLY-INDEX)
           TO   GRAND-TOTAL.
```

## Two Dimensional Arrays

| PASCAL | Java |
|---|---|
| General form for declaring a two-dimensional array<br><br>```
varName : array of array of type;
// Declares an array
SetLength(varName, size1);
// allocates memory for the array
SetLength(varName[i1], size2);
// where 0<=i1<=size1-1
```<br>or<br>```
varName : array [0..size1-1] of array [0..size2-1] of type
```<br><br>The following two lines create an array of 3 rows and 4 columns to hold 12 int values.<br><br>```
i : integer;
table : array of array of integer;
SetLength(table ,3);
for i := 0 to 2 do
  SetLength(table[i],4);
```<br>or<br>```
table : array [0..2] of array [0..3] of integer;
```<br><br>The valid indexes for the first dimension are from 0 to 2, for the second dimension from 0 to 3.<br><br>Examples:<br><br>```
y : Integer;
  :
  :
table[2][3] := 23;
y := table[1][3];
``` | General form for declaring two-dimensional array<br><br>```
type varName [][]; //declares an array
varName = new type[size1][size2];
         //allocates memory for the array
```<br><br>The following two lines create an array of 3 rows and 4 columns to hold int values.<br><br>```
int table[][];
table = new int[3][4];
```<br>or<br>```
int table[] = new int[3][4];
```<br><br>The valid indexes for the first dimension are from 0 to 2, for the second dimension from 0 to 3.<br><br>Examples:<br><br>```
table[2][3]=23;
int y = table[1][3];
``` |
```

## 42. Copying an Array

| FORTRAN | Visual Basic |
|---|---|
| Arrays can be copied by the simple assignment (=) statement.<br><br>`y = x`<br>    where `y` and `x` are arrays of same size | Arrays can be copied by simple assignment. The destination array should be a dynamic array. Visual Basic automatically allocates memory for the destination array and copies all the elements. |
| ```          INTEGER X(8), Y(8)          DATA X/5, 7, 12, 3, 4,     &         8, 9, 13/          Y=X          WRITE(*,*) Y(1),Y(8)          STOP          END``` | ```Private Sub Command1_Click()Dim x() As IntegerDim y() As IntegerReDim x(7)x(0) = 5: x(1) = 7: x(2) = 12: x(3) = 3x(4) = 4: x(5) = 8: x(6) = 9: x(7) = 13y = x  ' copies x() to y()Print y(0)Print y(7)End Sub``` |
| The output of the above program:<br><br>5     13 | The output of the above program:<br><br>5<br> 13 |

## Copying an Array

| C | Java |
|---|---|
| Arrays are copied one element at a time. | *System.arraycopy* method<br><br>*arraycopy(Object src, int srcPosition, Object dest, int destPosition, int elements)*<br><br>Copies an array from the specified source array, beginning at the specified position, to the specified position of the destination array |
| ```c
#include <stdio.h>
#include <malloc.h>
int main()
{
    int x[] = {5,7,12,3,4,8,9,13};
    int *y;
    int i;
    y = (int *) calloc(100 , sizeof(int));
    /* copy x into y */
    for (i = 91; i < 99; i ++)
       y[i] = x[i - 91];
     i = 91;
      printf("%d    %d\n",i,y[i]);
      i = 98;
      printf("%d    %d\n",i,y[i]);
    free(y);
    return 0;
}
``` | In the following example, all the 8 elements of the array x are copied to array y starting at the 91$^{st}$ position.<br><br>```java
class ArrayCopy{
    public static void main(String args[]){
         int x[] = {5,7,12,3,4,8,9,13};
         int y[] = new int[100];
         System.arraycopy(x, 0, y, 91, 8);
         i=91;
         System.out.println( i + "    "+y[i]);
         i=98;
         System.out.println( i + "    "+y[i]);
    }
}
``` |
| The output of the above program:<br><br>91    5<br>97    13 | The output of the above program:<br><br>91    5<br>97    13 |

167

## Copying an Array

### COBOL

Arrays are copied one element at a time.

```
        IDENTIFICATION DIVISION.
*-----------------------------------
        PROGRAM-ID. ARRCOPYP.
*-----------------------------------
*   This program copies specified
*   source-array beginning at the
*   specified position to the specified
*   position of the destination array.
*-----------------------------------
        ENVIRONMENT DIVISION.
        CONFIGURATION SECTION.
        DATA DIVISION.
        WORKING-STORAGE SECTION.
        01 ARRAY-1          PIC X(16)
            VALUES "0507120304080913".
        01 SOURCE-ARRAY REDEFINES ARRAY-1.
            05 SOURCE-ARRAY-ELEMENT PIC 99 OCCURS 8 TIMES.
        01 DESTINATION-ARRAY.
            05 DESTINATION-ARRAY-ELEMENT  PIC 99 OCCURS 100 TIMES.
        01 W-CNT            PIC 999 COMP VALUE 0.
        01 ARRAY-IND        PIC 99 COMP VALUE 0.
        01 DISPLAY-LINE.
            05 P-ARRAY-POS          PIC ZZ9BBBB.
            05 P-ARRAY-ELEMENT      PIC Z9.
*-----------------------------------
        PROCEDURE DIVISION
*-----------------------------------
        0000-MAIN.
*---------
            DISPLAY SPACES
            MOVE SPACES TO DISPLAY-LINE
            INITIALIZE DESTINATION-ARRAY.
            MOVE 1 TO ARRAY-IND.
            PERFORM MOVE-ARRAY THRU MOVE-ARRAY-EXIT
                VARYING W-CNT FROM 91 BY 1 UNTIL
                    W-CNT > 98.
            STOP RUN.
        0000-EXIT. EXIT.
        MOVE-ARRAY.
            MOVE SOURCE-ARRAY-ELEMENT (ARRAY-IND) TO
                DESTINATION-ARRAY-ELEMENT (W-CNT)
            MOVE W-CNT TO P-ARRAY-POS
            MOVE DESTINATION-ARRAY-ELEMENT (W-CNT) TO P-ARRAY-ELEMENT
            DISPLAY DISPLAY-LINE
            ADD 1 TO ARRAY-IND.
        MOVE-ARRAY-EXIT.  EXIT.
```

The output of the program:

```
91      5
92      7
93     12
94      3
95      4
96      8
97      9
98     13
```

## Copying an Array

| PASCAL | Java |
|---|---|
| Arrays are copied one element at a time. | `System.arraycopy` method<br><br>`arraycopy(Object src, int srcPosition, Object dest, int destPosition, int elements)`<br><br>Copies an array from the specified source array, beginning at the specified position, to the specified position of the destination array |

| PASCAL | Java |
|---|---|
| ```pascal
program ArrayCopy;
uses
  SysUtils;
var
  i : integer;
  x : array [0..7] of integer;
  y : array [0..99] of integer;
begin
x[0] :=5;x[1]:=7;x[2]:=12; x[3]:= 3;x[4]:=4;
x[5] := 8; x[6] :=  9; x[7] := 13;
  for i := 0 to 7 do
    y[i + 91] := x[i];  // Copy the array
    i :=91;
    Writeln(IntToStr(i)+' '+IntToStr(y[i]));
     i :=98;
    Writeln(IntToStr(i)+' '+IntToStr(y[i]));
end.
``` | In the following example, all the 8 elements of the array x are copied to array y starting at the 91[st] position.<br><br>```java
class ArrayCopy{
    public static void main(String args[]){
        int x[] = {5,7,12,3,4,8,9,13};
        int y[] = new int[100];
        System.arraycopy(x, 0, y, 91, 8);
        i=91;
        System.out.println( i + "   "+y[i]);
        i=98;
        System.out.println( i + "   "+y[i]);
    }
}
``` |
| The output of the above program:<br><br>91   5<br>97   13 | The output of the above program:<br><br>91   5<br>97   13 |

## 43. Formatting Numeric Output

| FORTRAN | Visual Basic |
|---|---|
| Numbers are formatted using editing descriptors like F, I, E, A, etc. | Use the `Format` function<br><br>*Format(expression, formatString)*<br>where<br>*expression* – expression to be formatted (numeric, date, time or string)<br>*formatString* – template to be used for formatting the expression to be returned |
| <pre>      INTEGER X, Y<br>      REAL*4 A, B, C<br>      X = 35<br>      Y = -2345<br>      A = .0457<br>      B = 35.49<br>      C = 1.5E-7<br>      WRITE(*,11) A<br>      WRITE(*,12) B<br>      WRITE(*,13) C<br>      WRITE(*,14) X<br>      WRITE(*,15) Y<br>11    FORMAT(' A = ',F8.3)<br>12    FORMAT(' B = ',F8.3)<br>13    FORMAT(' C = ',1PE12.3)<br>14    FORMAT(' X = ',I4.4)<br>15    FORMAT(' Y = ',I8)<br>      STOP<br>      END</pre> | <pre>Private Sub Command1_Click()<br>Dim x As Integer, y As Integer<br>Dim a As Double, b As Double, c As Double<br>x = 35: y = -2345<br>a = 0.0457: b = 35.49: c = 0.00000015<br>Print "a = " & Format(a, "0.000")<br>Print "b = " & Format(b, "0.000")<br>Print "c = " & Format(c, "0.00E+00")<br>Print "x = " & Format(x, "0000")<br>Print "y = " & Format(y, "#0")<br>End Sub</pre> |
| The output of the above program:<br><pre>A =     .046<br>B =   35.490<br>C =    1.500E-07<br>X = 0035<br>Y =    -2345</pre> | The output of the above program:<br><pre>a = 0.046<br>b = 35.490<br>c = 1.50E-07<br>x = 0035<br>y = -2345</pre> |

## Formatting Numeric Output

| C | Java |
|---|---|
| Formatting of the output is generally performed using the `printf()` function which uses various codes (`%d`, `%f`, etc) for formatting numbers and strings. | Use the format method of the *DecimalFormat* class<br>First create a pattern by using placeholders (0,#,E, etc) using the *DecimalFormat* object.<br>Then use the format method to convert a number to a string using the pattern created in the previous step |
| ```c<br>#include <stdio.h><br><br>int main()<br>{<br>    int x = 35, y = -2345;<br>    double a = 0.0457, b=35.49, c = 1.5e-7;<br>    printf("a = %.3lf\n", a);<br>    printf("b = %.3lf\n", b);<br>    printf("c = %.2E\n", c);<br>    printf("x = %04d\n", x);<br>    printf("y = %d\n", y);<br>    return 0;<br>}<br>``` | ```java<br>import java.text.*;<br>class Formatting{<br>    public static void main(String args[]){<br>    int x = 35, y=-2345;<br>    double a = 0.0457, b=35.49, c = 1.5e-7;<br>    DecimalFormat fmt1 = new DecimalFormat("0.000");<br>    System.out.println("a = "+fmt1.format(a));<br>    DecimalFormat fmt2 = new DecimalFormat("0.000");<br>    System.out.println("b = "+fmt2.format(b));<br>    DecimalFormat fmt3 = new DecimalFormat("0.00E00");<br>    System.out.println("c = "+fmt3.format(c));<br>    DecimalFormat fmt4 = new DecimalFormat("0000");<br>    System.out.println("x = "+fmt4.format(x));<br>    DecimalFormat fmt5 = new DecimalFormat("#0");<br>    System.out.println("y = "+fmt5.format(y));<br>    }<br>}<br>``` |
| The output of the above program:<br>`a = 0.046`<br>`b = 35.490`<br>`c = 1.50E-007`<br>`x = 0035`<br>`y = -2345` | The output of the above program:<br>`a = 0.046`<br>`b = 35.490`<br>`c = 1.50E-07`<br>`x = 0035`<br>`y = -2345` |

## Formatting Numeric Output

### COBOL

PICTURE clause used for displaying data in a required format.

```
       IDENTIFICATION DIVISION.
      *----------------------------------
       PROGRAM-ID. FORMATP.
       ENVIRONMENT DIVISION.
       CONFIGURATION SECTION.
       DATA DIVISION.
       WORKING-STORAGE SECTION.
       01 VARIABLES.
           05 VAR-X          PIC 99 VALUE 35.
           05 VAR-Y          PIC S9(4) VALUE -2345.
           05 VAR-A          PIC 9V9(4) VALUE  0.0457.
           05 VAR-B          PIC 99V99   VALUE 35.49.
           05 VAR-C          PIC 9V9(8) VALUE 0.00000015.
       01 DISPLAY-VARIABLES.
           05 DISPLAY-A      PIC 9.9(3).
           05 DISPLAY-B      PIC 99.999.
           05 DISPLAY-C      PIC 9.9(8).
           05 DISPLAY-X      PIC 9(4).
           05 DISPLAY-Y      PIC -9(4).
      *----------------------------------
       PROCEDURE DIVISION
       0000-MAIN.
      *---------
           DISPLAY SPACES
           COMPUTE   DISPLAY-A ROUNDED = VAR-A
           DISPLAY "A = " DISPLAY-A
           MOVE VAR-B TO DISPLAY-B
           DISPLAY "B = " DISPLAY-B
           MOVE VAR-C TO DISPLAY-C
           DISPLAY "C = " DISPLAY-C
           MOVE VAR-X TO DISPLAY-X
           DISPLAY "X = " DISPLAY-X
           MOVE VAR-Y TO DISPLAY-Y
           DISPLAY "Y = " DISPLAY-Y.
           STOP RUN.
       0000-EXIT. EXIT.
```

The output of the program:

```
A = 0.046
B = 35.490
C = 0.00000015
X = 0035
Y = -2345
```

## Formatting Numeric Output

| PASCAL | Java |
|---|---|
| Formatting of the output is performed by use of the format() function which formats the expression according to the specified template. | Use the format method of the *DecimalFormat* class. First create a pattern by using placeholders (0,#,E, etc) using the *DecimalFormat* object. Then use the format method to convert a number to a string using the pattern created in the previous step |

PASCAL:
```
program Formatting;
uses
  SysUtils;
var
  x, y     : Integer;
  a, b, c : double;
  fmt1, fmt2, fmt3, fmt4, fmt5 : string;
begin
  x := 35; y := -2345;
  a := 0.0457; b := 35.49; c := 1.5e-7;
  fmt1 := 'a = %0.3f';
  Writeln(format(fmt1,[a]));
  fmt2 := 'b = %0.3f';
  Writeln(format(fmt2,[b]));
  fmt3 := 'c = %0.3e';
  Writeln(format(fmt3,[c]));
  fmt4 := 'x = %0.4d';
  Writeln(format(fmt4,[x]));
  fmt5 := 'y = %d';
  Writeln(format(fmt5,[y]));
end.
```

Java:
```
import java.text.*;
class Formatting{
    public static void main(String args[]){
    int x = 35, y=-2345;
    double a = 0.0457, b=35.49, c = 1.5e-7;
    DecimalFormat fmt1 = new DecimalFormat("0.000");
    System.out.println("a = "+fmt1.format(a));
    DecimalFormat fmt2 = new DecimalFormat("0.000");
    System.out.println("b = "+fmt2.format(b));
    DecimalFormat fmt3 = new DecimalFormat("0.00E00");
    System.out.println("c = "+fmt3.format(c));
    DecimalFormat fmt4 = new DecimalFormat("0000");
    System.out.println("x = "+fmt4.format(x));
    DecimalFormat fmt5 = new DecimalFormat("#0");
    System.out.println("y = "+fmt5.format(y));
    }
}
```

The output of the above program (PASCAL):
```
a = 0.046
b = 35.490
c = 1.50E-007
x = 0035
y = -2345
```

The output of the above program (Java):
```
a = 0.046
b = 35.490
c = 1.50E-07
x = 0035
y = -2345
```

## 44. Converting between Different Data Types

| FORTRAN | Visual Basic |
|---|---|
| When assigning one type of data to another, automatic type conversion will always occur. The compiler does not do any type checking.<br><br>In the following example, a `double precision` is assigned to an `integer`. Unpredictable results will occur if the `double precision` value assigned is bigger than the capacity of the `integer`. | When assigning one type of data to another, automatic type conversion will always occur. The compiler does not do any type checking.<br><br>In the following example, a `Double` is assigned to an `Integer`. Unpredictable results will occur if the `Double` value assigned is bigger than the capacity of the `Integer`. |
| <pre>Integer x,i<br>Double Precision y,d<br>i=235<br>d=45.9<br>y=i<br>x=d<br>write(*,*) x<br>stop<br>end</pre> | <pre>Private Sub Command1_Click()<br>Dim I As Integer, X As Integer<br>Dim Y As Double, D As Double<br>I = 235<br>D = 45.9<br>Y = I<br>X = D<br>Print X<br>End Sub</pre> |
| The output of the program:<br><br>45 | The output of the program:<br><br>46 |

## Converting between Different Data Types

| C | Java |
|---|---|
| When assigning one type of data to another, automatic type conversion will always occur. The compiler does not do any type checking.<br><br>In the following example, a `double` is assigned to an `int`. Unpredictable results will occur if the `double` value assigned is bigger than the capacity of the `int`. | When assigning one type of data to another, automatic type conversion will occur if the two types are compatible and the destination type is larger than the source type<br><br>Cast is required to convert a larger type to a smaller type (when a potential loss of information is involved).<br><br>For example, an `int` can be assigned to a `double` but a cast is required to assign `double` to an `int`. |
| ```c
#include <stdio.h>
int main()
{
    int x;
    double y;
    int i=235;
    double d = 45.9;
    y = i;
    x = d;
    printf("%d\n",x);
}
``` | ```java
class Casting{
    public static void main(String args[]){
        int x;
        double y;
        int i=235;
        double d = 45.9;

        y = i;   // ok
        // x = d;      // not ok
        x = (int) d;
        System.out.println(x);
    }
}
``` |
| The output of the program:<br><br>46 | The output of the program:<br><br>45 |

**Converting between Different Data Types**

## COBOL

Cobol is not a strongly typed language. In Cobol, the type of a group item is always alpha-numeric. However, a variable defined at elementary level will have type determined by its picture clause. Cobol allows moving a character field to a numeric field. It is the responsibility of the programmer to manipulate data fields correctly.

## Converting between Different Data Types

| PASCAL | Java |
|---|---|
| When assigning one type of data to another, automatic type conversion will occur if the two types are compatible and the destination type is larger than the source type.<br><br>For example, an `Integer` can be assigned to a `Double` but use of the function `Trunc` is required to assign `Double` to an `Integer`. | When assigning one type of data to another, automatic type conversion will occur if the two types are compatible and the destination type is larger than the source type.<br><br>Cast is required to convert a larger type to a smaller type (when a potential loss of information is involved).<br><br>For example, an `int` can be assigned to a `double` but a cast is required to assign `double` to an `int`. |
| <pre>program Casting;<br>{$APPTYPE CONSOLE}<br>var<br>  x : Integer;<br>  y : Double;<br>  i : Integer = 235;<br>  d : Double = 45.9;<br>begin<br>  y := i;  // ok<br>  // x := d;    // not ok<br>  x := TRUNC(d);<br>  Writeln(x);<br>end.</pre> | <pre>class Casting{<br>    public static void main(String args[]){<br>        int x;<br>        double y;<br>        int i=235;<br>        double d = 45.9;<br><br>        y = i;  // ok<br>        // x = d;    // not ok<br>        x = (int) d;<br>        System.out.println(x);<br>    }<br>}</pre> |
| The output of the program:<br><br>45 | The output of the program:<br><br>45 |

## 45. Passing Arrays to Functions

| FORTRAN | Visual Basic |
|---|---|
| ```
      DIMENSION IX(11)
      DOUBLE PRECISION PROD
      DATA IX/7, 5, 6, 4, 10, 5,
     &        12, 23, 45, 3, 2/
      CALL PRODUCT(IX,11,PROD)
      WRITE(*,*) PROD
      STOP
      END
      SUBROUTINE PRODUCT(IY,ITEMS,P)
         DOUBLE PRECISION P
         DIMENSION IY(ITEMS)
         P=1
         DO I=1, ITEMS
            P=P*IY(I)
         END DO
         RETURN
      END
``` | ```
Private Sub Command1_Click()

Dim x(0 To 10) As Integer

x(0) = 7: x(1) = 5: x(2) = 6: x(3) = 4
x(4) = 10: x(5) = 5: x(6) = 12
x(7) = 23: x(8) = 45: x(9) = 3: x(10) = 2
Print Product(x)
End Sub

Function Product(y() As Integer)
   Dim i As Integer
   Product = 1
   For i = LBound(y) To UBound(y)
      Product = Product * y(i)
   Next i
End Function
``` |
| The output of the program:<br><br>3.129840000000000E+009 | The output of the program:<br><br>3129840000 |

## Passing Arrays to Functions

| C | Java |
|---|---|
| ```c
#include <stdio.h>

/* There is no way to determine the size of
the array from a pointer in C */
static double product(int a[], int size)
{
    double prod = 1;
    int i;
    for (i = 0; i < size; i ++)
    {
        prod = prod * a[i];
    }
    return prod;
}
int main()
{
    int x[] = {7,5,6,4,10,5,12,23,45,3,2};
    double prod;
    prod = product(x,sizeof(x)/sizeof(int));
    printf("%lf\n", prod);
    return 0;
}
``` | ```java
class PassingArray{
    public static void main(String args[]){

    int x[] = {7,5,6,4,10,5,12,23,45,3,2};
        System.out.println(product(x));
    }
    static long product(int a[]){
        long prod=1;
        for (int i=0; i<a.length; i++){
            prod = prod * a[i];
        }
        return prod;
    }
}
``` |
| The output of the program:<br><br>3129840000.00 | The output of the program:<br><br>3129840000 |

179

## Passing Arrays to Functions

### COBOL

```cobol
IDENTIFICATION DIVISION.
    PROGRAM-ID. PSARRAYP.
   * This program passes an integer array to a subprogram
   * which calculates the product of all elements the array
   * returns same to the calling program.
    ENVIRONMENT DIVISION.
    CONFIGURATION SECTION.
    DATA DIVISION.
    WORKING-STORAGE SECTION.
    01 WS-ARRAY.
       05 WS-FILLER            PIC X(22)
          VALUES "0705060410051223450302".
    01 DISPLAY-LINE .
       05 P-DISPLAY-RESULT  PIC Z(11)9.
    01 LINKED-BUFFER.
       05 LINKED-ARRAY      PIC X(22).
       05 LINKED-RESULT     PIC 9(12).
    PROCEDURE DIVISION    .
    0000-MAIN.
        DISPLAY SPACES.
        PERFORM CALL-PRODUCTP THRU CALL-PRODUCTP-EXIT.
        STOP RUN.
    0000-EXIT. EXIT.
    CALL-PRODUCTP.
        MOVE WS-ARRAY   TO LINKED-ARRAY.
        MOVE ZEROS      TO LINKED-RESULT
        CALL "PRODUCTP" USING LINKED-BUFFER
        MOVE LINKED-RESULT     TO P-DISPLAY-RESULT
        DISPLAY SPACES
        DISPLAY DISPLAY-LINE.
    CALL-PRODUCTP-EXIT.    EXIT.
```

```cobol
IDENTIFICATION DIVISION.
   *--------------------------------
    PROGRAM-ID. PRODUCTP.
   * This program returns the product of all element
   * of an array.
    ENVIRONMENT DIVISION.
    CONFIGURATION SECTION.
    DATA DIVISION.
    WORKING-STORAGE SECTION.
    77  WS-RESULT   PIC S9(12) COMP VALUE 0.
    01  WS-IND         PIC S99 COMP VALUE 0.
    LINKAGE SECTION.
    01  SUB-BUFFER .
        05 SUB-ARRAY            PIC 9(02) OCCURS 11 TIMES.
        05 SUB-RESULT           PIC 9(12).
    PROCEDURE DIVISION   USING SUB-BUFFER .
    0000-MAIN.
        MOVE 1      TO WS-RESULT
        PERFORM COMPUTE-PRODUCT THRU COMPUTE-PRODUCT-EXIT
             VARYING  WS-IND FROM 1 BY 1 UNTIL
                      WS-IND > 11.
        MOVE WS-RESULT   TO SUB-RESULT .
        GOBACK.
    0000-EXIT. EXIT.
    COMPUTE-PRODUCT.
             COMPUTE WS-RESULT = WS-RESULT * SUB-ARRAY(WS-IND).
    COMPUTE-PRODUCT-EXIT. EXIT.
```

The output of program:

3129840000

## Passing Arrays to Functions

| PASCAL | Java |
|---|---|
| ```pascal
program PassingArray;
{$APPTYPE CONSOLE}
uses
   SysUtils;

function product(a : array of Integer) :
Int64;
var
   i    : Integer;
   prod : Int64;
begin
   prod := 1;
   for i := 0 to Length(a) - 1 do
   begin
     prod := prod * a[i];
     Writeln(a[i], prod);
   end;
   result := prod;
end;
var
   x : array [0..10] of integer =
(7,6,5,4,10,5,12,23,45,3,2);
begin
   Writeln(IntToStr(product(x)));
end.
``` | ```java
class PassingArray{
   public static void main(String args[]){

   int x[] = {7,5,6,4,10,5,12,23,45,3,2};
      System.out.println(product(x));
}
static long product(int a[]){
      long prod=1;
      for (int i=0; i<a.length; i++){
          prod = prod * a[i];
      }
      return prod;
}
}
``` |
| The output of the program:<br><br>3129840000 | The output of the program:<br><br>3129840000 |

181

## 46. Program to Read Numbers from a Text File

| FORTRAN | Visual Basic |
|---|---|
| ``````fortran
      PROGRAM READTEXT
      REAL*4 XMAX, XMIN, X
      INTEGER COUNT
      XMAX = -1.7E38
      XMIN =  1.7E38
      COUNT=0
      OPEN(7, FILE='XYZ.DAT')
1     READ(7,*,END=99) X
      COUNT=COUNT+1
      IF (X. GT. XMAX) XMAX = X
      IF (X. LT. XMIN) XMIN = X
      GOTO 1
99    CONTINUE
      CLOSE(7)
      WRITE(*,*) 'Items = ',COUNT
      WRITE(*,*) 'Biggest = ',XMAX
      WRITE(*,*) 'Smallest = ',XMIN
      STOP
      END
``` | ```vb
Private Sub Command1_Click()
Dim max As Single
Dim min As Single
Dim x As Single
Dim count As Integer
Open "xyz.dat" For Input As 1
Do Until EOF(1)
   Input #1, x
   count = count + 1
   If (x > max) Then max = x
   If (x < min) Then min = x
Loop
Close 1
Print "Items = "; count
Print "Biggest = "; max
Print "Smallest = "; min
End Sub
``` |
| The output of the program:<br><br>```
Items =           101
Biggest =      6.503000E-01
Smallest =    -2.542000E-01
``` | The output of the program:<br><br>```
Items =  101
Biggest =  0.6503
Smallest = -0.2542
``` |

## Program to Read Numbers from a Text File

| C | Java |
|---|---|
| ```c
#include <stdio.h>
#include <limits.h>
#include <float.h>
int main()
{
    double max = -DBL_MAX;
    double min = DBL_MAX;
    double x;
    int count = 0;
    FILE *fin;
    fin = fopen("xyz.dat", "r");
    while ((fscanf(fin, "%lf", &x) != EOF))
    {
      //printf("x = %lf\n", x);
        count++;
        max = (x > max) ? x : max;
        min = (x < min) ? x : min;
    }
    fclose(fin);
    printf("Items    = %d\n",count);
    printf("Biggest  = %lf\n", max);
    printf("Smallest = %lf\n", min);
      return 0;
}
``` | ```java
import java.io.*;
class FindMaxMinFile {
  public static void main(String args[])throws IOException {
        String line;
        double max=-Double.MAX_VALUE;
        double min=Double.MAX_VALUE;
        double x;
        int count=0;
        FileInputStream fin = new FileInputStream("xyz.dat");
        BufferedReader inData = new BufferedReader(new InputStreamReader(fin));
        while((line = inData.readLine())!=null) {
            count++;
            //System.out.println(line+ " " + count);
            x = Double.parseDouble(line);
            max = (x > max) ? x : max;
            min = (x < min) ? x : min;

        }
        inData.close();
        System.out.println("Items    = " + count);
        System.out.println("Biggest = " + max);
        System.out.println("Smallest = " + min);
  }
}
``` |
| The output of the program:<br><br>```
Items    = 101
Biggest  = 0.6503
Smallest = -0.2542
``` | The output of the program:<br><br>```
Items    = 101
Biggest  = 0.6503
Smallest = -0.2542
``` |

## Program to Read Numbers from a Text File

### COBOL

```
        IDENTIFICATION DIVISION.
*-------------------------------
        PROGRAM-ID. FILEINP.
*-------------------------------
*   This program reads the file
*   containing numbers and prints
*   total no of entries ,MAX & minimum value .
*   The file is of text type with
*   sequential file organization
*-------------------------------
        ENVIRONMENT DIVISION.
        CONFIGURATION SECTION.
*SOURCE-COMPUTER. HP3000.
*OBJECT-COMPUTER. HP3000.
        INPUT-OUTPUT SECTION.
        FILE-CONTROL.

        SELECT OUTFILE              ASSIGN TO TEMP1
        FILE STATUS IS WS-STAT.
*-------------------------------
        DATA DIVISION.
*-------------------------------
        FILE SECTION.

        FD OUTFILE .
        01 OUTFILE-REC   .
            05 WS-NO              PIC SV9(4).
            05 FILLER             PIC X(6).
$PAGE "WORKING STORAGE Section"
*-------------------------------
        WORKING-STORAGE SECTION.
*-------------------------------
        01 WS-STAT            PIC XX VALUE SPACES.
        01 WS-COUNT           PIC 999 VALUE 0.
        01 WS-MIN             PIC SV9(4) VALUE 0.
        01 WS-MAX             PIC SV9(4) VALUE +0.9999.
        01 W-CNT              PIC 999 COMP VALUE 0.
        01 EOF                PIC X VALUE SPACES.
        PROCEDURE DIVISION.
        0000-MAIN.
            DISPLAY SPACES.
            OPEN INPUT   OUTFILE.
            IF WS-STAT <> "00"
               DISPLAY "ERROR OPENING FILE"
               STOP RUN.
            PERFORM READ-FILE THRU READ-FILE-EXIT.
            MOVE WS-NO TO WS-MIN     WS-MAX
            PERFORM PRINT-FILE THRU PRINT-FILE-EXIT
                UNTIL EOF EQUAL "Y".
            CLOSE OUTFILE
            DISPLAY "Items = "  WS-COUNT
            DISPLAY "Max   = "  WS-MAX.
            DISPLAY "Min   = "  WS-MIN.
            STOP RUN.
        0000-EXIT. EXIT.
        READ-FILE.
            READ OUTFILE AT END MOVE "Y" TO EOF.
            IF EOF <> "Y"
                ADD 1 TO WS-COUNT.
        READ-FILE-EXIT. EXIT.
        PRINT-FILE.
            IF (( WS-NO > WS-MAX ) OR   ( WS-NO = WS-MAX ))
                MOVE WS-NO  TO WS-MAX.
            IF (( WS-NO < WS-MIN ) OR   ( WS-NO = WS-MIN ))
                MOVE WS-NO TO WS-MIN.
            PERFORM READ-FILE THRU READ-FILE-EXIT.
        PRINT-FILE-EXIT. EXIT.
```

## Program to Read Numbers from a Text File

| PASCAL | Java |
|---|---|
| ```pascal
program FindMaxMinFile;
{$APPTYPE CONSOLE}
uses
   SysUtils;
const MAX_VALUE = 1.7E308;
var
   line       : string;
   max, min, x: double;
   count      : integer;
   fin        : TextFile;
begin
    max   := - MAX_VALUE;
    min   := MAX_VALUE;
    count := 0;
    AssignFile(fin, 'xyz.dat');
    Reset(fin);    // Move to beginning of file
    while not Eof(fin) do
    begin
        Readln(fin,line);
        Inc(count);
        //Writeln(line + ' ' + IntToStr(count));
        x := StrToFloat(line);
        if ( x > max ) then max := x;
        if ( x < min ) then min := x;
    end;
    CloseFile(fin);
    Writeln('Items    = ' + IntToStr(count));
    Writeln('Biggest  = ' + FloatToStr(max));
    Writeln('Smallest = ' + FloatToStr(min));
end.
``` | ```java
import java.io.*;
class FindMaxMinFile {
  public static void main(String args[])throws IOException {
        String line;
        double max=-Double.MAX_VALUE;
        double min=Double.MAX_VALUE;
        double x;
        int count=0;
        FileInputStream fin = new FileInputStream("xyz.dat");
        BufferedReader inData = new BufferedReader(new InputStreamReader(fin));
        while((line = inData.readLine())!=null) {
            count++;
            //System.out.println(line+ " " + count);
            x = Double.parseDouble(line);
            max = (x > max) ? x : max;
            min = (x < min) ? x : min;
        }
        inData.close();
        System.out.println("Items    = " + count);
        System.out.println("Biggest = " + max);
        System.out.println("Smallest = " + min);
   }
}
``` |
| The output of the program:<br><br>```
Items    = 101
Biggest  = 0.6503
Smallest = -0.2542
``` | The output of the program:<br><br>```
Items    = 101
Biggest  = 0.6503
Smallest = -0.2542
``` |

## 47. Program to Sort Numbers Using Shell Sort Algorithm

| FORTRAN | Visual Basic |
|---|---|
| ```
      Program ShellSort
      DOUBLE PRECISION TEMP
      INTEGER GAP
      LOGICAL DONE
      DOUBLE PRECISION DAT(10)
      DATA DAT/1.5, 3.5, 4.9, 2.2, 99.1,
     & 2.3, 0.1, 7.7, 8.4, 4.0/
      GAP=10/2
      DONE=.FALSE.
      DO WHILE (GAP.GE.1)
1       CONTINUE
        DONE=.TRUE.
        DO I=1,10-GAP
          IF(DAT(I).GT.DAT(I+GAP)) THEN
            TEMP=DAT(I)
            DAT(I)=DAT(I+GAP)
            DAT(I+GAP)=TEMP
            DONE=.FALSE.
          END IF
        END DO
        IF(.NOT. DONE) GOTO 1
        GAP=GAP/2
      END DO
      DO I=1,10
        WRITE(*,*) DAT(I)
      ENDDO
      STOP
      END
``` | ```
Private Sub Command1_Click()
Dim temp As Double
Dim I As Integer
Dim dat(9) As Double
Dim done As Boolean
Dim gap As Integer, Max As Integer
Max = 10
dat(0) = 1.5: dat(1) = 3.5: dat(2) = 4.9
dat(3) = 2.2: dat(4) = 99.1: dat(5) = 2.3: dat(6) = 0.1
dat(7) = 7.7: dat(8) = 8.4: dat(9) = 4#
gap = Max / 2
Do While (gap >= 1)
    Do
        done = True
        For I = 0 To Max - gap - 1
            If (dat(I) > dat(I + gap)) Then
                temp = dat(I)
                dat(I) = dat(I + gap)
                dat(I + gap) = temp
                done = False
            End If
        Next I
    Loop While (Not done)
    gap = Int(gap / 2)
Loop
For I = 0 To Max - 1
   Print dat(I)
Next I
End Sub
``` |
| Run the program. It will sort the numbers stored in the array. | Run the program. It will sort the numbers stored in the array. |

## Program to Sort Numbers Using Shell Sort Algorithm

| C | Java |
|---|---|
| ```c
#include <stdio.h>
#include <stdlib.h>
#define TRUE 1
#define FALSE 0
int main(int argc, char *argv[])
{
    double temp;
    int gap, done, I, K;
    double *data;
    if (argc < 2)
        return 1;
    data = (double *) malloc((argc - 1) * sizeof(double));
    for (i = 0; i < (argc - 1); i ++)
        data[i] = strtod(argv[i+1], (char **)NULL);
    gap = (argc - 1)/2;
    while (gap >= 1)
    {
        do
        {
            done = TRUE;
            for (i = 0; i < (argc - 1 - gap); i ++)
            {
                if (data[i] > data[i+gap])
                {
                    temp=data[i];
                    data[i]=data[i+gap];
                    data[i+gap]=temp;
                    done = FALSE;
                }
            }
        } while(!done);
        gap = gap/2;
    }
    printf("Sorted data:\n");
    for (k = 0; k < (argc - 1); k ++)
        printf("%lf ", data[k]);
    free(data);
    return 0;
}
``` | ```java
class ShellSort{
 public static void main(String args[]){
   if(args.length==0) return;
     double temp;
     int gap;
     boolean done;
     double data[] = new double[args.length];
     for (int i=0; i<args.length; i++) {
       data[i]=Double.valueOf(args[i]).doubleValue();
     }
     gap = args.length/2;

     while (gap>=1){
        do{
           done = true;
            for (int i=0; i<args.length-gap; i++){
               if (data[i]>data[i+gap]){
                   temp=data[i];
                   data[i]=data[i+gap];
                   data[i+gap]=temp;
                   done = false;
                } // end of if
            } // end of for
        } while(!done); //end of do.while
        gap = gap/2;
     } //end of while
     System.out.println("Sorted data:");
   for (int k=0; k<data.length; k++) {
     System.out.print(data[k]+ " ");
    }
  }//end of main
}
``` |
| Run the program by entering numbers as the command-line arguments. It will return those numbers sorted in the ascending order. | Run the program by entering numbers as the command-line arguments. It will return those numbers sorted in the ascending order. |

# Program to Sort Numbers Using Shell Sort Algorithm

## COBOL

```cobol
       IDENTIFICATION DIVISION.
       PROGRAM-ID. SHLSORTP.
      * This program reads the file containing
      * numbers and loads it in memory.
      * It then sorts them & prints.
       ENVIRONMENT DIVISION.
       CONFIGURATION SECTION.
       INPUT-OUTPUT SECTION.
       FILE-CONTROL.

           SELECT OUTFILE            ASSIGN TO TEMP1
           FILE STATUS IS WS-STAT.
           SELECT PRINT-FILE         ASSIGN TO PRINTOUT
           FILE STATUS IS WS-STAT.
       DATA DIVISION.
       FILE SECTION.

       FD OUTFILE .
       01 OUTFILE-REC   .
           05 WS-NO               PIC SV9(4).
           05 FILLER              PIC X(6).
       FD PRINT-FILE.
       01 PRINT-REC     .
           05 P-WS-NO             PIC -9.9999.
           05 FILLER              PIC X(3).
       WORKING-STORAGE SECTION.
       01 WS-STAT                 PIC XX VALUE SPACES.
       01 WS-ARRAY .
           05 WS-NO-A             PIC SV9999 OCCURS 200 TIMES.
       01 WS-TEMP-NO              PIC SV9999 VALUE ZEROS.
       01 WS-N                    PIC S999 VALUE 0.
       01 WS-I                    PIC S999 VALUE 0.
       01 WS-J                    PIC S999 VALUE 0.
       01 WS-K                    PIC S999 VALUE 0.
       01 WS-M                    PIC S999 VALUE 0.
       01 W-CNT                   PIC 999 COMP VALUE 0.
       01 WS-SORTED-FLAG          PIC X VALUE "N".
           88 SORTED              VALUE "Y".
           88 UNSORTED            VALUE "N".
       01 EOF                     PIC X VALUE SPACES.
       PROCEDURE DIVISION
       0000-MAIN.
           DISPLAY SPACES.
           OPEN INPUT   OUTFILE .
           IF WS-STAT <> "00"
              DISPLAY "ERROR OPENING OUTFILE"
              STOP RUN.
           OPEN OUTPUT PRINT-FILE.
           IF WS-STAT <> "00"
              DISPLAY "ERROR OPENING PRINT-FILE"
              STOP RUN.
           INITIALIZE WS-ARRAY.
           PERFORM READ-FILE THRU READ-FILE-EXIT.
           PERFORM FILL-ARRAY THRU FILL-ARRAY-EXIT
                   VARYING WS-N FROM 1 BY 1

                   UNTIL WS-N > 101  OR EOF EQUAL "Y".
           PERFORM SORT-DATA  THRU SORT-DATA-EXIT.
           PERFORM PRINT-DATA THRU PRINT-DATA-EXIT.
           CLOSE OUTFILE   PRINT-FILE.
       0000-EXIT. EXIT.
       READ-FILE .
            READ OUTFILE AT END MOVE "Y" TO EOF.
       READ-FILE-EXIT. EXIT.
       FILL-ARRAY.
            MOVE WS-NO  TO WS-NO-A(WS-N).
            PERFORM READ-FILE THRU READ-FILE-EXIT.
       FILL-ARRAY-EXIT.   EXIT.
       SORT-DATA .
            SET UNSORTED TO TRUE.
            MOVE WS-N TO WS-M
            PERFORM SORT-PROCEDURE VARYING WS-I FROM 1 BY 1
                        UNTIL WS-I = WS-N - 1
                        OR
                        SORTED.
            GO TO SORT-DATA-EXIT.
       SORT-PROCEDURE.
            SET SORTED TO TRUE
            COMPUTE WS-M = WS-M - 1
            PERFORM COMPARE-PAIRS
                    VARYING WS-J FROM 1 BY 1
                    UNTIL WS-J > WS-M.
       SORT-DATA-EXIT. EXIT.
       COMPARE-PAIRS.
            COMPUTE WS-K = 1 + WS-J
            IF WS-NO-A(WS-J) > WS-NO-A(WS-K)
               MOVE WS-NO-A(WS-J) TO WS-TEMP-NO
               MOVE WS-NO-A(WS-K) TO WS-NO-A(WS-J)
               MOVE WS-TEMP-NO TO WS-NO-A(WS-K)
               SET UNSORTED TO TRUE.
       PRINT-DATA.
            MOVE SPACES TO PRINT-REC.
            PERFORM WRITE-FILE THRU WRITE-FILE-EXIT
            VARYING WS-I FROM 1 BY 1 UNTIL WS-I > 101.
       PRINT-DATA-EXIT. EXIT.
       WRITE-FILE.
            MOVE SPACES TO PRINT-REC
            MOVE WS-NO-A(WS-I) TO P-WS-NO.
            WRITE PRINT-REC.
       WRITE-FILE-EXIT.   EXIT.
```

## Program to Sort Numbers Using Shell Sort Algorithm

### PASCAL

```pascal
program ShellSort;
{$APPTYPE CONSOLE}
Uses
  SysUtils;
var
  temp     : double;
  gap, i   : integer;
  done     : boolean;
  data     : array of double;
begin
  if ParamCount = 0 then exit;
  SetLength(data, ParamCount);
  for i := 0 to ParamCount - 1 do
  begin
    data[i] := StrToFloat(ParamStr(i+1));
  end;
  gap := TRUNC( ParamCount / 2 );
  while gap >= 1 do
  begin
    repeat
      done := true;
      for i := 0 to ParamCount - gap do
      begin
        if ( data[i] > data [i+gap] ) then
        begin
          temp        := data[i];
          data[i]     := data[i+gap];
          data[i+gap] := temp;
          done        := false;
        end;  // end of if
      end;  // end of for
    until NOT done;   // end of repeat..until
    gap := TRUNC( gap/2 );
  end;  // end of while
  Writeln ('Sorted data:');
  for i := 0 to Length(data) - 1 do
  begin
    Write( FloatToStr(data[i]) + ' ' );
  end;
end.
```

Run the program by entering numbers as the command-line arguments. It will returns those numbers sorted in the ascending order.

### Java

```java
class ShellSort{
 public static void main(String args[]){
  if(args.length==0) return;
    double temp;
    int gap;
    boolean done;
    double data[] = new double[args.length];
    for (int i=0; i<args.length; i++) {
      data[i]=Double.valueOf(args[i]).doubleValue();
  }
    gap = args.length/2;

    while (gap>=1){
      do{
         done = true;
          for (int i=0; i<args.length-gap; i++){
            if (data[i]>data[i+gap]){
               temp=data[i];
               data[i]=data[i+gap];
               data[i+gap]=temp;
               done = false;
            } // end of if
         } // end of for
      } while(!done); //end of do.while
       gap = gap/2;
    } //end of while
    System.out.println("Sorted data:");
   for (int k=0; k<data.length; k++) {
    System.out.print(data[k]+ " ");
   }
 }//end of main
}
```

Run the program by entering numbers as the command-line arguments. It will returns those numbers sorted in the ascending order.

## 48. Program to Compute the Leap Year

| FORTRAN | Visual Basic |
|---|---|
| ```
Program LeapYR
integer*2 year
logical leapYear
write(*,*) 'Enter 4 digit year'
read(*,*) year
if (mod(year,400).EQ.0) then
   leapYear=.TRUE.
else if (mod(year,100).EQ.0) then
   leapYear=.FALSE.
else if (mod(year,4).EQ.0) then
   leapYear=.TRUE.
else
   leapYear=.FALSE.
end if
if (leapYear) then
   write(*,*) year,' is a leap year'
else
   write(*,*) year,' is NOT a leap year'
end if
stop
end
``` | ```
Private Sub Command1_Click()
Dim Yr As Integer
Dim leapYear As Boolean
Yr = Val(Text1.Text)
If ((Yr Mod 400) = 0) Then
   leapYear = True
ElseIf ((Yr Mod 100) = 0) Then
   leapYear = False
ElseIf ((Yr Mod 4) = 0) Then
   leapYear = True
Else
   leapYear = False
End If
If (leapYear) Then
   Print "Year " & Yr & " is a leap year"
Else
   Print "Year " & Yr & " is NOT a leap year"
End If
End Sub
``` |
| Run the program and enter a 4-digit year when prompted. | Run the program and enter a 4-digit year in the text box. |

## Program to Compute the Leap Year

### C

```c
#include <stdio.h>

#include <stdlib.h>

#define TRUE 1
#define FALSE 0
int main(int argc, char *argv[])
{
    int leapYear;
    int year;
    if (argc < 2)
        return 1;
    year = atoi(argv[1]);

    if (year % 400 == 0) leapYear = TRUE;
    else if (year % 100 == 0) leapYear = FALSE;
    else if (year % 4 == 0) leapYear = TRUE;
    else leapYear = FALSE;

    if (leapYear)
        printf("The year %d is a leap year\n", year);
    else
        printf("The year %d is NOT a leap year\n", year);

    return 0;
}
```

```
C:\book\vcpp>LEAPYEAR 2100
The year 2100 is NOT a leap year

C:\book\vcpp>LEAPYEAR 1997
The year 1997 is NOT a leap year
```

### Java

```java
class LeapYear {
    public static void main (String args[]){
        if(args.length==0) return;
        int year = Integer.parseInt(args[0]);
        boolean leapYear;
        if (year%400 == 0) leapYear=true;
        else if (year % 100 == 0) leapYear = false;
        else if (year % 4 == 0) leapYear = true;
        else leapYear = false;
        if(leapYear) System.out.println("The year " +
                year + " is a leap year");
        else  System.out.println("The year " + year +
                        " is NOT a leap year");
    } // end of main
}
```

Run the program as follows:

```
D:\book\java>java LeapYear 2100
The year 2100 is NOT a leap year

D:\book\java>java LeapYear 1997
The year 1997 is NOT a leap year
```

## Program to Compute the Leap Year

### COBOL

```
        IDENTIFICATION DIVISION.
*------------------------------------
        PROGRAM-ID. LEAPYRP.
*------------------------------------
        AUTHOR.                  RADIP JOSHI.
        DATE-WRITTEN.            Jan 2000.
*------------------------------------
        ENVIRONMENT DIVISION.
        CONFIGURATION SECTION.
*------------------------------------
        DATA DIVISION.
*------------------------------------
        WORKING-STORAGE SECTION.
*------------------------------------
        01 ACCEPT-INPUT .
           05 ACCEPT-LEAP-YEAR     PIC 9999 VALUE 0.
           05 ACCEPT-LEAP-YEAR-R REDEFINES ACCEPT-LEAP-YEAR.
              10 ACCEPT-LEAP-YEAR-12    PIC 99 VALUE 0.
              10 ACCEPT-LEAP-YEAR-34    PIC 99 VALUE 0.
        77 NUM-REM              PIC 9999 VALUE ZEROS.
        77 NUM-REM1             PIC 9999 VALUE ZEROS.
*------------------------------------
        PROCEDURE DIVISION.
*------------------------------------

        0000-MAIN.
*---------
           DISPLAY SPACES.
           DISPLAY "Pl enter year in YYYY format"
           ACCEPT ACCEPT-LEAP-YEAR .
           IF ACCEPT-LEAP-YEAR-34 EQUAL ZEROS
              COMPUTE NUM-REM = FUNCTION REM (ACCEPT-LEAP-YEAR 400)
           ELSE
              MOVE ZEROS TO NUM-REM
           END-IF
           COMPUTE NUM-REM1 = FUNCTION REM (ACCEPT-LEAP-YEAR 4)
            IF NUM-REM EQUAL ZERO AND NUM-REM1 EQUAL ZERO
                DISPLAY ACCEPT-LEAP-YEAR , " is a leap year"
              ELSE
                DISPLAY ACCEPT-LEAP-YEAR , " is a not a leap year"
            END-IF.
              STOP RUN.
        0000-EXIT. EXIT.
```

## Program to Compute the Leap Year

### PASCAL

```
program LeapYear;
{$APPTYPE CONSOLE}
Uses
  SysUtils;
var
  year       : Integer;
  bLeapYear  : boolean;
begin
  if ParamCount = 0 then exit;
  year := StrToInt(ParamStr(1));
  if ( (year mod 400) = 0 ) then
    bLeapYear := true
  else if ( (year mod 100) = 0 ) then
    bLeapYear := false
  else if ( (year mod 4) = 0 ) then
    bLeapYear := true;
  if bLeapYear then
    Writeln('The year ' + IntToStr(year) +
' is a leap year')
  else
    Writeln('The year ' + IntToStr(year) +
' is NOT a leap year');
end.
```

### Java

```
class LeapYear {
    public static void main (String args[]){
        if(args.length==0) return;
        int year = Integer.parseInt(args[0]);
        boolean leapYear;
        if (year%400 == 0) leapYear=true;
        else if (year % 100 == 0) leapYear = false;
        else if (year % 4 == 0) leapYear = true;
        else leapYear = false;
        if(leapYear) System.out.println("The year " +
              year + " is a leap year");
        else  System.out.println("The year " + year +
                  " is NOT a leap year");
    } // end of main
}
```

Run the program as follows:

```
D:\book\pascal>LeapYear 2100
The year 2100 is NOT a leap year

D:\book\pascal>LeapYear 1997
The year 1997 is NOT a leap year
```

Run the program as follows:

```
D:\book\java>java LeapYear 2100
The year 2100 is NOT a leap year

D:\book\java>java LeapYear 1997
The year 1997 is NOT a leap year
```

## 49. Program to Generate Lotto Numbers

| FORTRAN | Visual Basic |
|---|---|
| ```
      Program LottoNumbers
      integer*4 current, ballsDrawn
      logical duplicate
      real*4 rand
      integer*4 ballsValue(100)
      ballsDrawn=0
      Write(*,*) 'Enter max value'
      read(*,*) biggest
      write(*,*) 'Enter no. of balls',
     x           ' to be drawn'
      read(*,*) balls
      do while(ballsDrawn .LT. balls)
         call Random(rand)
         current=int(biggest*rand) + 1
         duplicate=.FALSE.
         do i=1, ballsDrawn
            if (ballsValue(i).EQ. current) Then
               duplicate = .TRUE.
               exit
            end if
         end do
         if (.NOT.duplicate) then
            ballsDrawn = ballsDrawn +1
            ballsValue(ballsDrawn)=current
         endif
      end do
      Write(*,*) 'Here are the lotto numbers'
      write(*,1)(ballsValue(i),i=1,ballsDrawn)
    1 format(20I5)
      Stop
      End
``` | ```
Private Sub Command1_Click()
Dim I As Integer
Dim ballsValue() As Integer
Dim current As Integer
Dim ballsDrawn As Integer
Dim duplicate As Boolean
Dim biggest As Integer, balls As Integer
biggest = Val(Text1.Text)
balls = Val(Text2.Text)
ReDim ballsValue(balls - 1)
Do While (ballsDrawn < balls)
    current = Int(biggest * Rnd()) + 1
    duplicate = False
    For I = 0 To ballsDrawn - 1
        If (ballsValue(I) = current) Then
            duplicate = True
            Exit For
        End If
    Next I
    If (duplicate = False) Then
        ballsDrawn = ballsDrawn + 1
        ballsValue(ballsDrawn - 1) = current
    End If
Loop
For I = 0 To ballsDrawn - 1
    Print ballsValue(I)
Next I
End Sub
``` |
| Run the program, enter 51 and 6 when prompted. It will generate 6 random lotto numbers. | Run the program, enter 51 and 6 in the text boxes. It will generate 6 random lotto numbers. |

## Program to Generate Lotto Numbers

| C | Java |
|---|---|
| ```c
#include <stdio.h>

#include <stdlib.h>
#define TRUE 1
#define FALSE 0
int main(int argc, char *argv[])
{
    int i;
    int current;
    int duplicate;
    int ballsDrawn = 0;
    int biggest, balls;
    int *ballsValue;
    biggest = atoi(argv[1]);
    balls = atoi(argv[2]);
    ballsValue = (int *) malloc(balls * sizeof(int));
    while (ballsDrawn < balls)
    {
        current = (int) (biggest *
            ((double)rand()/RAND_MAX)) + 1;
        duplicate = FALSE;
        for (i = 0 ; i < ballsDrawn; i ++)
        {
            if (ballsValue[i] == current)
            {
                duplicate = TRUE;
                break;
            }
        }
        if (duplicate == FALSE)
        {
            ballsDrawn++;
            ballsValue[ballsDrawn-1] = current;
        }
    }
    printf("Here are the lotto numbers:");
    for (i = 0; i < ballsDrawn; i ++)
        printf("%d ", ballsValue[i]);
    free(ballsValue);
    return 0;
}
``` | ```java
class LottoNumbers {
    public static void main(String args[]) {
    int current;
    boolean duplicate;
    int ballsDrawn=0;
    int biggest = Integer.parseInt(args[0]);
    int balls = Integer.parseInt(args[1]);
      int ballsValue[] = new int[balls];
      while (ballsDrawn< balls) {
      current=(int)(biggest*Math.random())+1;
        duplicate = false;
        for (int i=0; i <ballsDrawn; i++) {
            if (ballsValue[i]==current) {
                duplicate = true;
                break;
            }
        }
        if (duplicate==false) {
            ballsDrawn++;
            ballsValue[ballsDrawn-
                    1]=current;
        }
    }
    System.out.print("Here are the"+
            "lotto numbers:");
    for (int i=0;i<ballsDrawn; i++)
        System.out.print(ballsValue[i]+ " ");
    }
}
```

**Run the program as follows:**

**java** LottoNumbers 51 6 |

## Program to Generate Lotto Numbers

### COBOL

```cobol
        IDENTIFICATION DIVISION.

        PROGRAM-ID. LOTTOP.
      * This program generates lotto numbers .

        ENVIRONMENT DIVISION.
        CONFIGURATION SECTION.
        DATA DIVISION.

        WORKING-STORAGE SECTION.

        77 RANDOM-NUMBER            PIC V99999 VALUE 0.
        01 ACCEPT-INPUT .
           05 WS-BIGGEST            PIC 99.
           05 WS-COUNTER            PIC 99.
        01 WS-ARRAY.
           05 ARRAY-ELM   PIC 99    OCCURS 6   TIMES.
        01 DISPLAY-LINE .
           05 P-DISPLAY-RESULT   PIC 99 OCCURS 6   TIMES.
        01 WS-IND                   PIC S99 COMP VALUE ZERO.
        01 WS-CNT                   PIC S99 COMP VALUE ZERO.
        01 DUPLICATE-FOUND-FLAG     PIC X VALUE SPACES.
           88 DUPLICATE-FOUND       VALUE "Y".
        01 WS-TEMP                  PIC 99 VALUE 0.
        01 TEMP-VAR.
           05 WS-TEMP1-X            PIC X(7) VALUE SPACES.
           05 WS-TEMP1-N REDEFINES WS-TEMP1-X   PIC 9(7).
           05 WS-TEMP1-N-V REDEFINES WS-TEMP1-X PIC 99V99999.
           05 WS-LOTTO-NO-W         PIC 99.9(6).
           05 WS-LOTTO-NO REDEFINES  WS-LOTTO-NO-W .
              10 WS-LOTTO-NO-INT    PIC 99.
              10 WS-REST            PIC X(7).
        01 WS-IND-2                 PIC S99 COMP VALUE 0.

        PROCEDURE DIVISION.

        0000-MAIN.
       *---------
           DISPLAY SPACES.
           DISPLAY "P1 Input the biggest number & no of iteration"
           ACCEPT ACCEPT-INPUT.
           INITIALIZE WS-ARRAY
           MOVE 1 TO WS-IND-2
           PERFORM CALL-LOTTO     THRU CALL-LOTTO-EXIT
                    VARYING WS-IND FROM 1 BY 1
                    UNTIL WS-IND  > WS-BIGGEST
           DISPLAY SPACES.
           MOVE WS-ARRAY TO DISPLAY-LINE.
           DISPLAY DISPLAY-LINE.
           STOP RUN.
        0000-EXIT. EXIT.
        CALL-LOTTO.
           COMPUTE RANDOM-NUMBER = FUNCTION RANDOM
           COMPUTE WS-TEMP1-N-V ROUNDED = (RANDOM-NUMBER * WS-BIGGEST)
                                        + 1.
           MOVE SPACES TO DUPLICATE-FOUND-FLAG.
           MOVE WS-TEMP1-X(1:2) TO WS-LOTTO-NO-INT
           MOVE WS-LOTTO-NO-INT TO WS-TEMP
           PERFORM SEARCH-DUPL VARYING WS-CNT FROM 1 BY 1
                    UNTIL WS-CNT > 6
           IF NOT DUPLICATE-FOUND
              MOVE WS-TEMP TO ARRAY-ELM (WS-IND-2)
              ADD 1 TO WS-IND-2.
        CALL-LOTTO-EXIT.   EXIT.
        SEARCH-DUPL.
             IF WS-TEMP = ARRAY-ELM (WS-CNT)
                MOVE "Y" TO DUPLICATE-FOUND-FLAG.
```

**Program to Generate Lotto Numbers**

| PASCAL | Java |
|---|---|
| ```
program LottoNumbers;
{$APPTYPE CONSOLE}
Uses
  SysUtils;
var
  I, current, ballsDrawn,biggest,balls : Integer;
  duplicate  : boolean;
  ballsValue : array of Integer;
begin
  ballsDrawn := 0;
  biggest    := StrToInt(ParamStr(1));
  balls      := StrToInt(ParamStr(2));
  SetLength(ballsValue,balls);
  while (ballsDrawn < balls) do
  begin
    current    := TRUNC(random(biggest)) + 1;
    duplicate := False;
    for i := 0 to ballsDrawn - 1 do
    begin
      if (ballsValue[i] = current) then
      begin
        duplicate := true;
        break;
      end;
    end;
    if duplicate = false then
    begin
      Inc(ballsDrawn);
      ballsValue [ballsDrawn-1] := current;
    end;
  end;
  Write('Here are the Lotto Numbers: ');
  for i := 0 to ballsDrawn - 1 do
  begin
    Write(IntToStr(ballsValue[i]) + ' ');
  end;
end.
``` | ```
class LottoNumbers {
    public static void main(String args[]) {
    int current;
    boolean duplicate;
    int ballsDrawn=0;
    int biggest = Integer.parseInt(args[0]);
    int balls = Integer.parseInt(args[1]);
      int ballsValue[] = new int[balls];
      while (ballsDrawn< balls) {
      current=(int)(biggest*Math.random())+1;
          duplicate = false;
          for (int i=0; i <ballsDrawn; i++) {
              if (ballsValue[i]==current) {
                  duplicate = true;
                  break;
              }
          }
          if (duplicate==false) {
              ballsDrawn++;
              ballsValue[ballsDrawn-
                      1]=current;
          }
      }
    System.out.print("Here are the"+
              "lotto numbers:");
    for (int i=0;i<ballsDrawn; i++)
        System.out.print(ballsValue[i]+ " ");
    }
}
``` |
| Run the program as follows:<br><br>`LottoNumbers 51 6` | Run the program as follows:<br><br>`java LottoNumbers 51 6` |

## 50. Program to Generate Character-based Bar Graph

| FORTRAN | Visual Basic |
|---|---|
| ```
program Graph
integer*4 graphData(10)
integer*4 i,j, MaxData
write(*,*) 'Enter values, -1 to end'
do i=1,10
    Read(*,*) graphData(i)
    if (graphData(i).LT.0) exit
    MaxData=MaxData+1
end do
do i=1, MaxData
    do j=1, graphData(i)
        write(*, '(a\)') ' *'
    end do
    write(*,*)
end do
stop
end
``` | ```
Private Sub Command1_Click()
Dim GraphData(4) As Integer
Dim str As String
Dim K As Integer, I As Integer
For K = 0 To 4
str = InputBox("Enter the bar value", , "0")
    GraphData(K) = CInt(str)
Next K
For K = 0 To 4
    For I = 1 To GraphData(K)
        Print "*";
    Next I
    Print
Next K
End Sub
``` |
| Run the program, enter 3,5,7,2,12, -1 when prompted.<br><br>The output of the program:<br><br>\*\*\*<br>\*\*\*\*\*<br>\*\*\*\*\*\*\*<br>\*\*<br>\*\*\*\*\*\*\*\*\*\*\*\* | Run the program, enter 3,5,7,2 when prompted.<br><br>The output of the program:<br><br>\*\*\*<br>\*\*\*\*\*<br>\*\*\*\*\*\*\*<br>\*\* |

## Program to Generate Character-based Bar Graph

### C

```c
#include <stdio.h>
#include <stdlib.h>
#include <malloc.h>
int main(int argc, char *argv[])
{
    int *graphData;
    int i, k;
    if (argc < 2)
        return 1;
    graphData =(int *)malloc((argc-1) * sizeof(int));
    for (i = 0; i < (argc-1); i ++)
        graphData[i] = atoi(argv[i+1]);
    for (k = 0; k < (argc-1); k ++)
    {
        for (i = 1; i <= graphData[k]; i++)
        {
            printf("*");
        }
        printf("\n");
    }
    free(graphData);
    return 0;
}
```

Run the program as follows:

```
D:\book\C>jGraph 3 5 7 2 12 8
***
*****
*******
**
************
********
```

### Java

```java
class Graph {
    public static void main (String args[]){
        if(args.length==0) return;
        int graphData[] = new int[args.length];
        for (int i=0; i<args.length; i++) {
            graphData[i]=Integer.parseInt(args[i]);
        }
        for (int k=0; k<graphData.length; k++) {
            for (int i=1; i<=graphData[k]; i++) {
                System.out.print("*");
            }
            System.out.print("\n");
        }
    } // end of main
}
```

Run the program as follows:

```
D:\book\java>java Graph 3 5 7 2 12 8 3
***
*****
*******
**
************
********
***
```

# Program to Generate Character-based Bar Graph

## COBOL

```cobol
        IDENTIFICATION DIVISION.
*------------------------------------
        PROGRAM-ID. GRAPHP.
*------------------------------------
*------------------------------------
*   This program draws a graph.
*------------------------------------
        ENVIRONMENT DIVISION.
        CONFIGURATION SECTION.
*------------------------------------
        DATA DIVISION.
*------------------------------------
        WORKING-STORAGE SECTION.
*------------------------------------
        01  ACCEPT-INPUT .
            05 ACCEPT-INPUT-NO    PIC 99 OCCURS 7 TIMES

        01  DISPLAY-LINE.
            05 PRINT-CHAR    PIC X OCCURS 60 TIMES.
        01  W-CNT            PIC S99 COMP VALUE 0.
        01  WS-IND           PIC S99 COMP VALUE 0.

*------------------------------------
        PROCEDURE DIVISION .
*------------------------------------
        0000-MAIN.
*---------
            DISPLAY SPACES.
            DISPLAY "Enter 7 integer "
            ACCEPT ACCEPT-INPUT.
            DISPLAY SPACES.
            PERFORM PRINT-GRAPH THRU PRINT-GRAPH-EXIT
                    VARYING  W-CNT FROM 1 BY 1 UNTIL
                             W-CNT > 7.
            STOP RUN.
        0000-EXIT. EXIT.
        PRINT-GRAPH.
         MOVE SPACES TO DISPLAY-LINE
         MOVE 1 TO WS-IND
         PERFORM WRITE-CHAR VARYING WS-IND FROM 1 BY 1
             UNTIL WS-IND > ACCEPT-INPUT-NO(W-CNT)
             DISPLAY DISPLAY-LINE.
        PRINT-GRAPH-EXIT.    EXIT.
        WRITE-CHAR.
             MOVE "*" TO PRINT-CHAR(WS-IND).
```

### The output of the program:
```
Enter 7 integer
03050702120803

***
*****
*******
**
***********
*******
***
```

## Program to Generate Character-based Bar Graph

| PASCAL | Java |
|---|---|
| ```pascal
program graph;
{$APPTYPE CONSOLE}
Uses
  SysUtils;
var
  i, k       : Integer;
  graphData  : array of Integer;
begin
  if ParamCount = 0 then exit;
  SetLength(graphData,ParamCount);
  for i := 0 to ParamCount - 1 do
  begin
    graphData[i] := StrToInt(ParamStr(i+1));
  end;
  for k := 0 to Length(graphData) - 1 do
  begin
    for i := 0 to graphData[k] - 1 do
    begin
      Write('*');
    end;
    Writeln('');
  end;
end.
``` | ```java
class Graph {
    public static void main (String args[]){
        if(args.length==0) return;
        int graphData[] = new int[args.length];
        for (int i=0; i<args.length; i++) {
            graphData[i]=Integer.parseInt(args[i]);
        }
        for (int k=0; k<graphData.length; k++) {
            for (int i=1; i<=graphData[k]; i++) {
                System.out.print("*");
            }
            System.out.print("\n");
        }
    } // end of main
}
``` |
| **Run the program as follows:**<br><br>D:\book\pascal>Graph 3 5 7 2 12 8 3<br>\*\*\*<br>\*\*\*\*\*<br>\*\*\*\*\*\*\*<br>\*\*<br>\*\*\*\*\*\*\*\*\*\*\*\*<br>\*\*\*\*\*\*\*\*<br>\*\*\* | **Run the program as follows:**<br><br>D:\book\java>java Graph 3 5 7 2 12 8 3<br>\*\*\*<br>\*\*\*\*\*<br>\*\*\*\*\*\*\*<br>\*\*<br>\*\*\*\*\*\*\*\*\*\*\*\*<br>\*\*\*\*\*\*\*\*<br>\*\*\* |

## CD ROM CONTENTS

| Product | Contained in folder | To use or install |
|---|---|---|
| JDK 1.2.2 | JDK | run *jdk1_2_2-001-win.exe* |
| JDK Documentation | JDKDoc | open *jdk1_2_2-001-doc.zip* |
| TextPad® Editor | TextPad | run *txpeng41.exe* |
| Adobe® Acrobat® Reader | AR | run *rs405eng.exe* |
| IBM VisualAge for Java Entry Edition | IBMVA | run *setup.exe* |
| *Thinking in Java*, *First Edition* by Bruce Eckel | TIJ1 | Open *Contents.html* using a browser |
| *Thinking in Java*, *Second Edition* by Bruce Eckel | TIJ2 | Open *Contents.html* using a browser |
| Java Coding Conventions Document | JCC | Open using *CodeConventions.pdf* Acrobat Reader |
| Java Language Environment White Paper | JLEWP | Open using *langenviron.pdf* Acrobat Reader |
| Source Code for the book | BookSRC | Open corresponding folders containing Visual Basic, FORTRAN, Java, Pascal, Cobol and C code. |

System Requirements: Windows 95, 98 or NT

## LICENSE AGREEMENT AND LIMITED WARRANTY

By opening the sealed software package, you accept and agree to the terms and conditions printed below and in the full printed license agreement. If you do not agree, do not open the package.

The software is distributed on an "as is" basis, without warranty. Neither the author, the software developers, nor Engineering Mechanics Technology, Inc. makes any representation, or warranty, either express or implied, with respect to the software programs, their quality, accuracy or fitness for specific purpose. Therefore, neither the author, the software developers, nor Engineering Mechanics Technology, Inc shall have any liability to you or any other person or entity with respect to any liability, loss or damage caused directly or indirectly by the programs contained on the media. This includes, but not limited to service, loss of data or consequential damages from the use of these programs. If the media itself is defective, you may return it for replacement.

Licensed Materials – IBM® VisualAge® for Java$^{TM}$, Entry Edition for Windows® 95, Windows® 98, and Windows NT®, Version 3.0.
© Copyright IBM Corp. 1991, 2000, and by others. All Rights Reserved.
US Government Users Restricted Rights – Use, duplication or disclosure of VisualAge for Java is restricted by GSA ADP Schedule Contract with IBM Corporation.

IBM and VisualAge are trademarks of IBM Corp. in the U.S. and/or other countries.
Java and all Java-based trademarks and logos are trademarks or registered trademarks of Sun Microsystems, Inc. in the United States and other countries.
Windows is a trademark of Microsoft Corporation in the U.S. and/or other countries.

VisualAge for Java